INSIGHT COMPACT GUIDE

Venice

Compact Guide: Venice is a culture-based guide for a culture-based destination, revealing the splendours of the city's monuments, the wealth of its churches and museums and the delights of its bridges and canals.

This is one of over 100 titles in Insight Guides' series of pocket-sized, easy-to-use guidebooks intended for the independent-minded traveller. Compact Guides are in essence travel encyclopedias in miniature, designed to be comprehensive yet portable, as well as up-to-date and authoritative.

Star Attractions

An instant reference to some of Venice's most popular tourist attractions to help you on your way.

Piazza San Marco p15

Bronze horses at San Marco p17

Doge's Palace p24

Canal Grande p33

Scala Contarini del Bovolo p41

Equestrian statue of Colleoni p44

Rialto Bridge p47

Frari Church p53

Tintoretto works p55

Chioggia p80

Venice

Venice – Wonder of the World

In the popular imagination, Venice offers a kaleidoscope of images, from romantic gondolas to garish Murano glassware, from crumbling palaces on the Grand Canal to masked revellers at the Venetian Carnival. Summer presents the bustling splendour of Piazza San Marco while winter is swathed in mystery: the mist-laden, monochrome curtain of a city out of season. Then, the city conjures up the cultivated melancholy of Visconti's haunting *Death in Venice*, based on Thomas Mann's novel.

Any gloom is soon dispelled by a fishy risotto or *risi e bisi* (rice with peas). Luminous Venetian painting embraces Canaletto's stately majesty, Titian's vibrant explosions of colour and Tintoretto's mastery of light and shadow. Private Venice harbours its own pleasures, from secluded backwaters to mildewed churches or the soporific sound of boat horns drifting over the canals.

The coat of arms

For more than a millennium, the Republic of Venice used all its strength to repel unwelcome invaders. Today it welcomes the foreign hordes with open arms: one of the world's greatest maritime powers has become one of the world's greatest tourist attractions. Its sheer uniqueness makes it a wonder of the world. No other Western city has so many historic buildings built on water; few other cities have so successfully straddled East and West, with glittering architectural treasures from both worlds.

Venice needed no structural alterations in order to accommodate modern traffic; cars simply have to turn back once they reach Piazzale Roma. As a result, Venice is unsullied by modernity, an act of foresight on the part of the city's founders. Not for nothing is Venice known as La Serenissima, the 'most serene' city, the title bestowed on it by its Republican rulers.

Location and size

Situated at the northwestern end of the Adriatic Sea, Venice lies on an archipelago in a crescent-shaped lagoon some 51km (32 miles) in length. At 1 metre (3.2ft) above sea-level, Greater Venice stands on 118 islets in this shallow lagoon. The city of Venice itself is linked by 160 canals and criss-crossed by over 600 bridges.

The shallow waters of the Venetian lagoon are protected from the open sea by the Litorale del Cavallino promontory in the north, the Chioggia-Sottomarina promontory in the south, and in between are a line of sandbanks or *lidi*. These sandy islets are home to small settlements, of which the best known is the Lido, built as a fashionable seaside resort in the 19th century.

Like natural sluices, the three gaps of Porto di Lido, Porto di Malamocco and Porto di Chioggia all connect

The rooftops of Venice

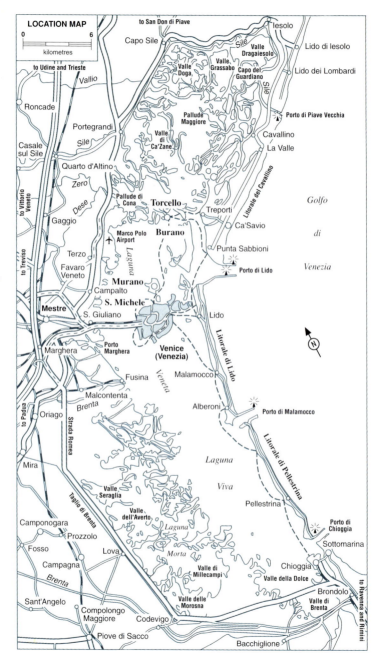

LOCATION MAP

0   6
kilometres

to San Don di Piave

Capo Sile

Iesolo

Sile

Valle
Dragaiesolo

Lido di Iesolo

Lido dei Lombardi

to Udine and Trieste

Vallio

Valle
Doga

Valle
Grassabo

Capo del
Guardiano

Roncade

Portegrandi

Pallude
Maggiore

Sile

Casale
sul Sile

Sile

Quarto d'Altino

Zero

Valle
di
Ca'Zane

Porto di Piave Vecchia

Cavallino

La Valle

Litorale del Cavallino

to Vittorio
Veneto

Dese

Pallude di
Cona

Torcello

Treporti

Golfo

Gaggio

Marco Polo
Airport

Burano

Ca'Savio

di

Terzo

Laguna

Punta Sabbioni

Venezia

to Treviso

Favaro
Veneto

Murano

Campalto

S. Michele

Porto di Lido

6

Mestre

S. Giuliano

Lido

Marghera

Porto
Marghera

Venice
(Venezia)

Litorale di Lido

N

Fusina

Veneta

Malamocco

to Padua

Oriago

Malcontenta

Brenta

Alberoni

Porto di Malamocco

Mira

Strada Romea

Taglio di Brenta

Laguna

Viva

Litorale di Pellestrina

Camponogara

Valle
Seraglia

Pellestrina

Porto di
Chioggia

Prozzolo

Valle
dell'Averto

Sottomarina

Fosso

Lova

Laguna

Campagna

Morta

Chioggia

Brenta

Valle di
Millecampi

Valle della Dolce

Sant'Angelo

Compolongo
Maggiore

Valle delle
Morosna

Brondolo

Valle di
Brenta

to Ravenna and Rimini

Codevigo

Piove di Sacco

Bacchiglione

with the sea, which is essential for shipping as well as for the lagoon's ecological balance. But the sea also represents a threat to Venice because of the risk of high tides; the last devastating flood was in 1966.

Venice's strategically unique position resulted in the development of an equally unique city within the lagoon. Harbours that had silted up, such as the one at Ravenna, further south on the Adriatic, made the Venetians realise the dangers that threatened their own city, and they soon redirected the Brenta, Sile and Piave rivers with estuaries in the lagoon. Such medieval foresight meant that Venice never silted up, and remained a port.

Rise of a maritime power

Cut off from the mainland, its secure position guaranteed, and facing out towards the sea and the East, Venice developed a brisk, long-distance trade with Byzantium, a relationship which flourished from the 5th century onwards. The city exported salt, fish and ships, and imported sought-after consumer goods in return: spices, silks and exotic luxuries. The craft traditions of Byzantium, unchanged since antiquity, catered to the needs of Europe's medieval masters via the Venetian clearing house. The city also manufactured its own glassware and built ships for trade and war.

Securing the shipping routes brought coastal fortifications and colonisation in its wake. Venice controlled the islands of Rhodes, Cyprus, Crete and Corfu, with Corfu remaining Venetian until the end of the Republic in 1797. Marco Polo (1254-1324), the great Venetian adventurer, travelled throughout the Far East and helped open up trading links between Asia and the West. As for trade with the Black Sea and North Africa, the safe harbours of Koron and Modon at the southern exit of the Adriatic were known as the 'Eyes of the Republic'.

In its heyday, Venice ruled the Adriatic and the eastern Mediterranean. In 1420 it was the richest city in the world, and 200 years later, after the lion's share of territorial possessions had gone to Turkey, Venice still possessed more wealth than the great powers of Central Europe. It was this prosperity that led to such a flowering of the arts in the 17th and 18th centuries, after the initial Renaissance bloom had faded.

Long before the fall of Constantinople (1453) Venice had been expanding across to the mainland, creating neighbouring colonies and distant caravan routes. It was almost as if it sensed the impending loss of its maritime trade; the Peace of Lodi (1454) secured it the routes across the Alps and into Central Italy. Nevertheless, the discovery of the New World created new patterns of trade, and Venice was ultimately sidelined.

Naval symbol outside the Museo Storico Navale

The Cannaregio Canal

The Doge's Palace

The Doges and their Republic

None of Venice's burgeoning power would have been possible without the security engendered by the Venetian Republic. The Republic, run by an unbroken line of doges for over a thousand years, represented the rock beneath the shifting sands of Venetian fortunes. The role of doge (from the Latin dux, leader or duke) was an institutionalised version of a Byzantine governorship. The position was not hereditary, thus removing the threats posed by monarchy or feudalism.

Instead, the doge acted as the public representative of enlightened patrician rule, a position which gradually evolved into a figurehead role. The doges, backed by the checks and balances provided by the Republican constitution, oversaw a period of great prosperity and artistic patronage. Until its abolition in 1797, the Venetian constitution occupied a unique place in European history, at once the staunch defender of the ruling class and the guarantor of civic duty.

Legacy of a world power

Venice was a world maritime power for centuries, and the effects are obvious, from the magnificent Doge's Palace to the late Byzantine flowering of San Marco. This was a cosmopolitan city of Levantine, Bohemian, Greek and Slav merchants. Architecturally, too, Venice became a melting-pot, with a bias for Byzantine richness over Renaissance purity of line. The palaces flanking the Grand Canal were built over a span of around 500 years.

As far as house construction was concerned, Venice set a precedent: the floor of each palazzo was open, because the city's secure location made fortifications unnecessary. On the ground floor, where boats were moored, was the warehouse; above was the *piano nobile*, the main floor, graced with *saloni* and anterooms. Standing sentinel outside the palazzi are *paline*, the mooring poles bedecked in the colours of the original patrician residents.

Ground-floor parking

In financial matters, Venice was the acknowledged world leader and has bequeathed us much basic banking terminology. Many expressions commonly used in Venetian trade with the Orient also found their way into European languages, including such words as arsenal, coffee, ghetto, magazine and marzipan.

Venice in peril

The centuries-old problem of Venice sinking was halted by measures taken in the 1970s against industrial communities disturbing the balance of the lagoon. But the city is still plagued by other problems, ranging from pollution from the industrial zones of Mestre and Marghera to flooding and depopulation. A further blow to the city's image has been the destruction of the Fenice opera house by fire in January 1996. This jewel of an opera house will rise again, as it did after the fire of 1836, but inevitably it will divert funds from other vital projects.

Venice has always been threatened by floods: the combination of an area of low pressure in Northern Italy, a strong southeasterly wind and simultaneous tides can send masses of water from the Adriatic into the lagoon. On 14 November 1966 the city was flooded for 13 hours up to a depth of nearly 2m (6.5ft). An appeal was launched, and in 1992 the government finally freed funds for the so-called 'Progetto Mosè' (Moses Project) involving the construction of huge mobile flood protection barriers at the Porto di Lido, Porto di Malamocco and Porto di Chioggia. However, after assessment by a team of international experts concerning its viability, the controversial project was put on hold by the government at the end of 1998 and its future now hangs in the balance.

Water markers

Venice today

Venice is by no means a living museum. The inhabitants are noted for their tricky dialect, fierce independence, sense of irony and stoical approach. Theirs is a spirit borne out of the slow pace of Venetian life and a lingering nostalgia for past greatness. It is personified by the sultry yet cool Venetian aristocracy or the offhand approach of the city gondoliers. Yet this public mask also conceals a carnivalesque temperament, a sense of fun which is given free rein at festivals.

9

Carnival masks

In its heyday, the city of Venice boasted 200,000 inhabitants, a figure which fell to 90,000 at the end of the Republic. By 1995 the population had dwindled to a mere 73,000, pinpointing an exile which is not entirely voluntary: curiously, this city of absentee landlords does not offer enough rental accommodation, and flats are too expensive for most locals. Building restoration costs in Venice are also almost double those of mainland Mestre. As a consequence, more Venetians are moving to Mestre and commuting to work. While Venice lives off industry on the mainland, its islands depend on tourism.

Over seven million tourists visit every season so Venice has long toyed with the idea of introducing a quota system. However, the majority of visitors depart in the evening, with barely two million staying overnight. This is a time when the city breathes again. Yet out of season Venice has much to offer, apart from the riotous pre-Lenten Carnival. Venice is just as intriguing in winter, retaining the cheerful attitude to life that is so characteristic of its inhabitants. And in the murky depths of winter fogs, what better way to restore cheer than a *grappa*, the famous drink originally distilled in Venice.

Tourists on Piazza San Marco

Historical Highlights

The first inhabitants of the region came from the Aegean; itinerant farmers, hunters and fishermen, they led a simple life and built houses on stilts. Their incorporation into the Roman Empire went smoothly. Difficulties faced by archaeologists excavating the lagoon, however, have made it hard to prove conclusively that it was inhabited at that time. Place names do strongly suggest, though, that the lagoon must have had a lively infrastructure of its own and must already have been settled before the peoples of the mainland fled there from the invading armies at the end of the Roman Empire.

From the 5th century onwards Huns, Goths, Ostrogoths, Lombards and Franks all streamed across the Alps into the Friulian Plain, and Venice was also made an outpost of Byzantium after the Eastern (Byzantine) Empire had gained a foothold in Italy.

The Venetians did not want foreign rule, and saw themselves being squeezed back into the central area of the lagoon: their earlier towns of Aquilea, Oderzo, Grado and Eraclea had all been destroyed, and in 742 the seat of power, which had been represented by a doge (duke) since 697, was shifted to Malamocco on the island of Lido.

After surviving the dangers of a Frankish invasion in 809, led by Pepin, the son of Charlemagne, the government of the young state on the Rialto stabilised once more. Rivus Altus (Rialto), in a secure position 2km (1 mile) from the mainland and 2km from the open sea, became the heart of the Republic. The legendary date of its foundation, 25 March 421, despite being celebrated annually, is inaccurate; Rivus Altus was replaced by the name Venezia (Venice) only in the 13th century. The Rialto group of islands still forms the heart of this trading city; its administrative centre was shifted in 828, after the acquisition of the relics of St Mark, to where the Doge's Palace and San Marco basilica stand today.

In 814, a Franco-Byzantine treaty guaranteed Venice political and juridical independence from the rule of the Western Empire, without implying any dependence on Byzantium. The city's spirit of fierce independence bore fruit. Venice was open to the sea and to trade with Byzantium, and the treasures of the East began to arrive, including silk, ivory and spices.

The coastline was still dangerous, however, and Venice finally controlled the Dalmatian coast only by the year 1000. With the safety of the shipping routes assured, and with the support of Byzantine interests in Southern Italy, the young maritime power negotiated further privileges until it was autonomous. The way was clear for Venice, situated as it was between the Eastern (or Byzantine) Empire and the new lords in the West, beyond the Alps, to become a world power.

Role of the Republic

Venice, the youngest republic in Italy, was succesfully ruled by doges from 697 onwards. As the young state grew more powerful, maintaining power became a central concern. In 1172 the Maggior Consiglio, or Great Council, was formed, with membership limited to the city's patrician families. The Council, led by the elected doge, remained an elected body until 1297, when membership became hereditary. The dreaded Consiglio dei Dieci (Council of Ten) was introduced as a security measure after the Tiepolo/Querini conspiracy of 1310 and ruled through intimidation; it was assisted by the Quarantia, a 40-member Supreme Court.

Venice's independence from the West saved it from feudalism, and its internal constitution spared it from becoming a monarchy. The Venetian state, unique in Europe, lasted until 1797 and was ruled by a total of 120 doges.

697 The first doge is elected. The Venetian fleet is the largest in the Adriatic.

1082–5 Victory over the Normans, who posed a threat to Venetian access to the Adriatic.

1094 San Marco is consecrated.

1177 Venice intercedes in the controversy between the Emperor and the Pope: Barbarossa and Alexander III meet in San Marco.

1202–4 The Fourth Crusade ends with the capture of Constantinople; Venice uses power politics against the Sultan of Egypt and attains the height of its colonial power: it controls three-eighths of the Byzantine Empire, the Cyclades and Crete, and shipping routes as distant as the Black Sea.

1271 Marco Polo (1254–1324) sets out from Venice for China. He wrote *Il Milione* (The Travels of Marco Polo) as a prisoner of war in Genoa. The Venetian merchant went on what could be termed the first adventure holiday – though it lasted a full quarter of a century. At the age of 17, he left his native city and travelled via Baghdad, Persia (Iran) and Afghanistan to reach the court of the Mongol prince Kublai Khan. As the prince's close adviser, he then travelled throughout the Far East and helped open up trading links between Asia and the West.

13th–14th century War with its great rival, Genova (Genoa), for the control of shipping routes. The creation of *scuole*, the charitable confraternities or guilds which bestowed so much on the city in terms of artistic patronage.

1378–81 The Battle of Chioggia ends with Genoa's defeat. The Peace of Turin reaffirms Venetian supremacy.

15th century Venice expands on to the mainland; trading routes are secured across the Alps and into Central Italy.

1453 The Ottomans conquer Constantinople; trading routes with the Orient are cut off.

1454 The Peace of Lodi: Venice secures the routes across the Alps and into Central Italy. Its territory now comprises the Po Valley, Lake Garda, the Alps and Istria.

1492 The loss of Black Sea trade is followed by the discovery of America.

1498 The sea route to India via the Cape of Good Hope is discovered; Venice no longer monopolises trade with India and declines as a world power.

16th century Venice prospers during the 16th and 17th centuries, acting as a trade clearing house between Europe and Asia. This is the golden age of Venetian painting, with Giovanni Bellini (1430–1516), Titian (1488–1576), Tintoretto (1518–94) and Veronese (1528–88).

1508–9 The 'League of Cambrai'. Envious of Venice's position, France, Spain, the Emperor, the Pope and the Italian city-states form a deadly alliance against Venice. Territorial losses are minimised via clever diplomacy, but Venice still loses its Italian hegemony and mainland colonies.

1570 Cyprus falls to the Turks. Venice and the Western powers defeat the Turks at the Battle of Lepanto (1571), but this alters nothing.

17th century The House of Habsburg (Austrian and Spanish line) and the threat from Turkey remain the two polarising forces in Venetian politics. Venice lives on its accumulated wealth.

1718 Peace of Passarowitz: Venice relinquishes all its colonial possessions; Austria and Turkey reach an agreement. Venice is no longer a world power, but a mere state. Its famed autonomy and neutrality also render it vulnerable to attack.

18th century Venice becomes a city of adventurers and gamblers. The city's top families stay wealthy, but a lack of pioneering spirit results in decadence – accurately portrayed by writers Giacomo Casanova and Carlo Goldoni and the genre painters Pietro Longhi (1702–84), Francesco Guardi (1712–93) and Canaletto (1697–1768).

1797 The Napoleonic army surrenders Venice without a fight to its arch-enemies, the Habsburgs.

1805 Venice becomes part of Napoleon's Kingdom of Italy.

1815 The Congress of Vienna returns Venice to Austria.

1848–9 Venice succeeds in driving out its Austrian rulers for months.

1866 The Peace of Vienna: Austria guarantees a referendum which results in Venice being ceded to Italy. Venice thus loses its autonomy.

1915 Italy declares war on Austria; the Venetian mainland becomes a World War I battleground.

1946 Foundation of the Republic of Italy.

1958 Giuseppe Roncalli, Patriarch of Venice, rules as Pope John XXIII until 1963.

1966 Venice is severely damaged by floods.

1994 The 400th anniversary of Tintoretto's death.

1995 Centenary of Biennale Exhibition.

1996 La Fenice opera house destroyed by fire.

1998 The Mosè (Moses) Project to save Venice from floods is blocked by the government.

Piazza San Marco

Preceding pages: view from the Campanile

Route 1

Piazza San Marco – San Marco Basilica – Doge's Palace

Connoisseurs insist that the best way to approach San Marco for the first time is by water; if this isn't possible, there is also a very good view to be had when entering the arcades of the **Ala Napoleonica** ❶ (those not on foot should disembark at the San Marco-Calle Vallaresso landing-stage), where the least attractive part of the entire complex is at your back. There was a gap in the architecture there right up until 1810, when Napoleon ordered it to be closed – he referred to St Mark's Square as the 'finest drawing-room in all Europe', but still felt that a rear wall had to be added after all.

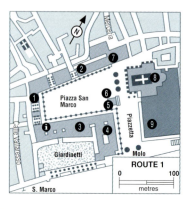

Staircase of the Museo Correr

This Napoleonic wing today contains the entrance to the **Museo Correr** (April to October, daily 9am–7pm; November to March, daily 9am–5pm; ticket includes entrance to Palazzo Ducale, Museo Vetrario in Murano and Museo dei Merletti in Burano). The collection here includes cultural and historical artefacts (documents, costumes, coins), an art gallery (Italian and Flemish masters from the 14th to the 17th century) and also the special Museo di Risorgimento section, documenting the resistance against Austrian occupation during the 19th century until Venice was reunited with Italy in 1866.

The two wings of the building on the north side of the piazza are known as the *procuratie*, formerly the offices of the city's most important administrative officials, the procurators. On the site of the previous building here, which was Byzantine in style, the **Procuratie Vecchie** (Old

Procurators' Offices) **②** were built between 1480 and 1517. Designed by Mauro Coducci, they were constructed by Bartolomeo Bon. The arcades still have a Byzantine flavour; the arches are not imitation, but actually an Early Renaissance novelty. Scamozzi started on the construction of the **Procuratie Nuove** (New Procurators' Offices) **③**, opposite, in 1582, and the building was completed by Longhena around 1640. The Procuratie Nuove were not modelled on Byzantium but instead on the **Libreria Vecchia** (Old Library) **④** just around the corner. In 1537 Florentine architect Jacopo Sansovino had wanted to build it *alla romana*; the plan that Scamozzi completed after Sansovino's death and transferred to his own new building marked a turning-point in Venetian architecture; the Byzantine and Gothic styles had served their purpose, and the classically-oriented ideals of the Renaissance were now coming into their own. The Old Library has a long, graceful facade arcaded on two storeys; the richly decorated frieze is pierced by attic windows. This new formal language introduced by Sansovino became an object of study not only in Venice but all over Europe.

Arcades of the Procuratie Vecchie

The library is well worth visiting during temporary exhibitions or by appointment (tel: 5208788); the staircase with its white and gold stucco emulates the Scala d'Oro in the Doge's Palace (*see page 27*); on the ceiling is Titian's fresco of *Wisdom*. The Sala Dorata (Golden Hall) has a gold ceiling separated into seven sections, each containing three medallions: seven painters had a contest here, supervised by Titian, and the winner was Paolo Veronese (6th row). Five of the 12 paintings of philosophers on the walls are by Tintoretto (four hang on the wall facing the courtyard, the fifth is on the rear wall). The glass cases contain the most valuable of the Old Library's ancient books; there are 750,000 altogether, and they are stored in the former Zecca (Mint), the wing facing the Molo. The antique collections, bequeathed to the city in 1523 by Cardinal Grimani, were also housed in Sansovino's new building; the entrance to the Museo Archeologico is to the right of the Library's main portal (closed for restoration).

15

The Loggetta

The **Loggetta ⑤**, with its three arches and ornate attic, resembles a rather over-wide Roman city gate, and is also by Sansovino. Towering above it is the **Campanile ⑥**, (June to September, daily 9.30am–10pm; October to May 9.30am–4.15pm). The oldest structure in the square, it was begun in the 9th century; after several construction phases between the 12th and 14th century, the 98-m (322-ft) high tower was completed in 1514. On 14 July 1902 the campanile collapsed, causing little damage to other buildings and no human casualties; its reconstruction was officially opened on St Mark's Day (25 April) in 1912. The view from the campanile across the lagoon is justly famous.

Three imposing-looking flagstaffs stand in front of the church: this is where the flag of St Mark used to fly, and is still hoisted during festivals. The bronze pedestals are the work of Alessandro Leopardi (1505).

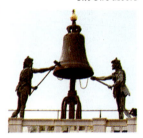

The Two Moors

A popular sight are the *due mori* (Two Moors), the bronze figures who strike the hours up on the **Torre dell'Orologio** (Clock Tower) ❼. Coducci had originally planned the tower as the final section of his Procuratie Vecchie, and the bronze figures of the Two Moors were cast in 1497, as was the clock, which shows not only the time of day but also the phases of the moon and the passage of the sun through the zodiac. The lion in front of the stars was added in 1755, along with the upper storey. When the tower reopens after restoration the public will have access to the upper balcony.

The domes of San Marco

★★★ St Mark's Basilica (San Marco) ❽

Open: Basilica, Pala d'Oro, Treasury, Gallery and Museum Monday to Saturday 9.45am–4.30pm, Sunday 1.30–4.30pm; admission fees for Pala d'Oro, Treasury, Gallery and Museum and last entry 30 minutes before closing.

History

In the year 828, Venice successfully stole the relics of St Mark from Alexandria; Venetian legend has it that Mark the Evangelist regained consciousness on an island in the lagoon after a shipwreck, having been addressed in a dream by an angel with the words *Pax tibi, Marce evangelista meus. Hic requiescet corpus tuum* (Peace be with you, Mark, my Evangelist. This will be your final resting-place) – thus conveniently justifying the young state's claim to the relics.

The first San Marco basilica was consecrated in 832; the fire in 976 (ignited by the dissatisfied populace against a tyrannical doge) that burnt down the Doge's Palace also damaged part of the structure, and in 978 the second San Marco basilica was built on the same site. Today's building, however, is 'Mark 3', as it were, the so-called 'Contarini church'.

In 1063 a rather expensive new building was started, and was consecrated in 1094. It was modelled after the Church of the Apostles in Constantinople – later destroyed by the Turks when they captured the city – and its ground plan was a Greek cross with four arms of equal length. At the front was a narthex with a two-storey facade divided up into five arcades, the middle ones of which were emphatically decorated as the main portal. The reconstruction conveys the austerity of the originally highly Byzantine facade of San Marco.

The two-storey facade

The city's rapid rise to power after the success of the Fourth Crusade (*see page 10*) allowed the facade to be

16

adapted to contemporary taste in the 13th century, namely Romanesque; the carrier sections of the lower arcades were replaced by playful double pillars which break up the facade. More booty from Byzantium followed in the shape of the four ★★★ **bronze horses** on the loggia (they are actually copies; the originals are in the museum); then the baptistery and St Isidore's chapel were added, as were the domes. The appearance of the facade at that time has been preserved in the mosaic of the first arcade on the left.

Bronze horses

During the first half of the 15th century the facade was adorned with some Gothic icing: pointed arches made the arcades higher, sculpted figures and narrow towers all reflect the soaring quality of the Gothic style. The building's brick exterior was faced with fine marble and decorated with select works of art brought to Venice from all over the world.

A mixture of styles, magnificently coloured and majestic, the San Marco basilica has undergone very few significant alterations over the past 500 years or so. The merchant republic of Venice had done its patron saint – whose dominions far and near were symbolised by the winged lion of St Mark – fitting honour at the height of its power, and the basilica became the Chiesa d'Oro, the Golden Church. Throughout the duration of the Republic it was the seat of the doge and of secular power; the patriarch of Venice has resided in San Marco only since 1807.

17

A bronze door

Exterior
Five doorways lead from the front of the building into the narthex; four of them have bronze doors, the fifth (on the corner by the Doge's Palace) is glass. The main facade is in two orders, each of five arches, with the emphasis on the central arch, the main portal. Its ★ **bronze doors** with their lions' heads came from Byzantium in the 11th

Flags of St Mark

Last Judgement mosaic

century. The main outer arch has 14th-century carvings showing Venetian trades – in sharp contrast to the *Last Judgement*, a neoclassical mosaic that was added in only 1836. The sculpture decoration below is Romanesque (12th- and 13th-century) and depicts the Months (soffit), the Virtues and Beatitudes (outer face), and symbolic representations of animals (smallest arch). In the lunette is an expressive Romanesque marble carving of the *Dream of St Mark* (13th-century).

Portal columns

The side portals are also richly decorated, with mosaics showing how the relics of St Mark were brought to Venice; the mosaic on the far left is the only one dating from the time the basilica was built (1260–70). It is the earliest known representation of the building's exterior, and the bronze horses are already in place.

The north facade, facing the Piazzetta dei Leoncini, was probably the last to be finished. The first arch has a 7th-century relief of Christ and the 12 disciples as lambs; a bas-relief between the first two arches shows Alexander the Great being transported to heaven by two griffins (10th-century Byzantine). All three arches are decorated with an assortment of geometrical figures and mysterious animals and shapes.

The last of the four arches is the 13th-century Porta dei Fiori (Flower Portal); the beautifully carved pointed arches enclose a nativity scene – a masterpiece of Venetian Romanesque. Beyond the projecting wall here is the porphyry sarcophagus of Daniele Manin, who led the rebellion against Austrian rule that was crushed in 1849. Manin died in exile in Paris in 1857, and his ashes were brought to Venice in 1868.

At the southwest corner of the facade is the Pietra del Bando, a stump of a porphyry column from which the decrees of the Signoria were promulgated from 1256 onwards – a counterpart to the Gobbo di Rialto (Hunchback of Rialto, *see page 49*). The south facade, formerly open to the Molo, has been closed for some time now because of the reconstruction of the Cappella Zen. Between the two upper arches is a 13th-century Byzantine mosaic of the Madonna in prayer. The two isolated pillars in front of the baptistery door, with their oriental motifs, are a rare example of Syrian carving of the 4th century.

Mosaic of the Madonna

The massive wall that leads to the Doge's Palace is decorated with polychrome marble intarsia; there may once have been a fortified tower on this site, forming part of the old Doge's fortress. The sculptured group on the corner – carved from porphyry – is known as the *Tetrarchi*. The four figures (4th-century Egyptian) are thought to represent Diocletian and three other Roman emperors (late 3rd-century).

After the surfeit of decoration around the basilica it is refreshing to take a few steps in the direction of the Loggetta, to turn around when halfway there and to look back up at the domes: above the south facade there are still traces of the original brick walls, giving an idea of how the strictly Byzantine structure in the 11th century must once have looked.

19

Interior

The centre doorway leads into the **narthex** (atrium), which originally lined three sides of the church's actual interior; the side facing the Piazzetta was closed and was given a new liturgical function as the Cappella Zen and the baptistery. The oldest part, which dates back to the beginning of the building under Doge Domenico Selvo (1071–84), can be seen in the section containing the elaborate central doorway: the austere pillars, arches, niches and mosaics betray their Byzantine origin. The bronze doors are early 12th-century, and were modelled after the ones on the right-hand portal (11th-century Byzantine). The bronze door in front of the Cappella Zen [Y] resembles the central doorway on the exterior facade: Byzantine art (6th-century). The ★ **intarsia floors** of the narthex are 11th- and 12th-century; in front of the centre portal, a red marble slab marks the spot where Barbarossa did obeisance before Alexander III in 1177, at the height of the investiture controversy. The *St Mark in Ecstasy* mosaic (1545) in the semi-dome is the work of Francesco and Valerio Zuccato, based on a sketch by Lorenzo Lotto. The ceiling of the narthex was originally flat; the domes were vaulted in the 13th century, which is also when the mosaic floor was added. The mosaics of the domes and arches are

The intarsia floors

The domes and arches

ST. MARK'S

0   20

metres

on themes taken from the Old Testament:
[A] *Creation and the Fall of Man*, [B] the
Story of Noah and the Flood, [C] the *Tower
of Babel*, [D] the *Story of Abraham*, [E]
the *Story of Joseph*, [F] *Joseph is Sold to
Potiphar*, [G] *Joseph Rules Egypt*, [H] the
Story of Moses. The mosaics here in the
narthex clearly reveal how Venetian artists
succeeded in freeing themselves from the
severity and formality of the Byzantine tradition, and developed their own dynamic
and highly imaginative mosaic style.

Before leaving the Narthex and entering the interior of San Marco proper, the numerous pillars should not be missed: their
capitals are miniature masterpieces.

The ★★ **interior** of the basilica is breathtaking: the interplay of the domes and
arches creates a dynamic rhythm, while the actual shape
of the ground plan with its four arms of equal length ar-
rests this architectural movement and calms it again – San
Marco is a compelling and harmonious blend of the dynamic and the static, of tranquillity and movement. Before any details can be distinguished, one is almost dazzled
by the apparently infinite number of mosaics on their gold
backgrounds – covering over 4,000sq m (43,000sq ft) of
space.

One of the mosaics

The pictorial representations are placed around the
building according to the original medieval iconograph-
ical scheme: beneath Christ, high in the cupola, are the angels and Apostles, with the *Story of St Mark*, and the pillars
and arches are then decorated down to ground level with
stories of various select saints.

The main Dome of the Ascension [I] shows Christ being carried by four angels, and Mary by two; the 12 Apostles frame the picture. The 16 Virtues of Christ are depicted
in the windows; the four Evangelists are in the four
pendentives. The dome above the altar [II] shows the Re-
ligion of Christ as foretold by the Prophets; the Virgin
stands between Isaiah and Daniel; the symbol of the four
Evangelists can be seen in the spandrels.

In the Dome of the Pentecost [III] the mosaics depict
the Triumph of Faith: here we see the Descent of the Holy
Spirit, with tongues of fire inspiring the 12 Apostles and,
between the windows, the Converted Nations; in the pendentives, four enormous angels. The mosaics in these three
12th-century domes are artistically the most valuable.
Breaks in style in San Marco have been unavoidable, however, since several of the mosaics had to be renewed over
the centuries and, many have been redone in the style of
the 16th and 17th centuries.

I Above the centre portal, *the Saviour between the Virgin and St Mark* (13th-century, restored); in the arch, *Scenes from the Apocalypse* (16th-century and modern); also a *Last Judgement* based on sketches by Jacopo Tintoretto (16th-century).

J *The Passion*, from the Kiss of Judas until the Crucifixion (13th-century).

K *Scenes from the Life of Christ*, based on sketches by Jacopo Tintoretto (16th-century).

L *The Passion, the Agony in the Garden, Deeds of the Apostles* (13th-century).

M *Christ and the Apostles; the Deeds of the Apostles* (13th to 16th-century).

N *Christ Pantocrator*, based on sketches by Tintoretto (16th-century).

O *Scenes from the Life of Christ* (12th–13th-century).

P *Deeds of John the Evangelist*; in the centre, a Greek cross; the *four Fathers of the Church* in the pendentives (late 12th-century).

Q Several saints particularly popular with the Venetians: *St Nicola, St Clemente, St Biagio, St Leonardo* (13th-century).

Christ, the Virgin and St Mark

Christ in benediction

21

The many art treasures in St Mark's, whether plundered, donated or made in Venice, are concentrated in the choir around the presbytery (*presbiterio*); it is somewhat higher than the rest of the church because of the crypt (*cripta*) beneath it. The ★ **iconostasis** separates the priests from the ordinary people. The liturgical reform of the second Vatican Council (1962–4) placed a rather ugly wooden podium in front of the screen so that Mass could be celebrated 'closer to the people' – however, the podium hides almost all the stylobate with its 16 marble arches, from the previous 10th-century church. The artistic polychrome marble structure is crowned by a series of sculptures: grouped around the dominant cross in the middle are the *Virgin, St John the Evangelist and the 12 Apostles* – a work by Jacobello and Pierpaolo Delle Masegne (1394). On the right platform made of porphyry and marble, supported by nine pillars of various exotic marbles, the newly-elected doge was presented to the public. On the left-hand side are two ★ **pulpits**: the lower, octagonal one has an impressive marble parapet and is supported by 11 pillars, and the higher one is remarkable for its design: seven narrow columns support the pulpit which consists of five cylindrical posts; above it, on six red marble columns, is a little Oriental cupola.

The pillars

To the right of the iconostasis, the way leads inside the choir; the two tribunes opposite one another with bronze reliefs by Sansovino (16th-century) were for singers and musicians. The high altar gained its present-

Sun on the bronze lamps

The altar by Bartolomeo Bon

day appearance from the restoration phase of 1834–6. The four ★★ **columns** supporting the baldachin are particularly delightful: they are decorated with sculpture from top to bottom, with motifs taken from the Life of Christ and of the Virgin; their origin is uncertain, and they have been dated between the 6th and 13th century. The altarpiece provides a view of the sarcophagus of St Mark; the bronze lamps are 16th-century. Beyond the high altar is the unique ★★★ **Pala d'Oro**, with its precious stones, old gold and enamel, which was originally planned to go in front of the altar. Doge Pietro Orseolo (876–78) commissioned it in Constantinople; over five centuries it was enlarged and enriched. It is 3.48m (11.4ft) long and 1.4m (4.6ft) high. The frame dates from the time of its creation; the six *Scenes from the Life of Christ* in the upper section came from Byzantium in 1209. The lower section is the work of Venetian artists (1345): in the centre, the Pantocrator, surrounded by the four Evangelists and flanked by three rows of Prophets, Apostles and Angels. Square niches with enamels, worked in the *cloisonné* technique, depict episodes from the lives of Christ, the Virgin and St Mark (1105). Each part of the Pala d'Oro is decorated with priceless gems. This is one of the most remarkable works ever produced by medieval goldsmiths.

The apse of St Mark's has three niches: the altar in the middle one is decorated by four spiral-shaped columns, and the tabernacle by Sansovino bears a bronze relief of the Saviour; the remarkable sacristy door in the left-hand niche is also by Sansovino; and through the golden grille in the right niche, the doge could watch the church unobserved. The mosaic in the apse shows Christ Pantocrator (1506). The saints between the windows below, however, are remains of mosaics dating from the time the church was first built (11th century).

R Cappella di Sant'Isidoro (St Isidore's chapel). 14th-century mosaics illustrating the life of St Isidore; Gothic altar (14th-century) containing the saint's relics.

S ★ **Cappella della Madonna dei Mascoli**. 15th-century mosaics illustrating the *Life of the Virgin*; the altar by Bartolomeo Bon is encased in splendid marble.

T Mosaics illustrating the *Life of the Virgin* (12th- and 13th-century).

U Cappella della Madonna Nicopeia. A 10th-century icon of the Virgin, taken to Venice after the sack of Constantinople in 1204; the name means 'victory-bringer'.

V Altare del Sacramento. An eternal flame stands as a reminder that the relics of St Mark were found again after the fire of 976; the floor mosaic shows where they were found in 1094.

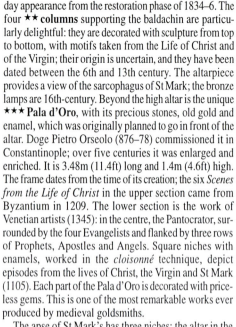

W In the nave pier, a large bas-relief of *Madonna con Bambino* (Madonna and Child, also known as *Madonna del Bacio*, Madonna of the Kiss, since it has been worn away by the kisses of the faithful). On the side wall opposite is the door leading to the Tesoro (Treasury) [Z], with an attractive ogee arch above it.

X Battistero (Baptistery). Font designed by Sansovino (1546) with reliefs (Evangelists; *Scenes from the Life of John the Baptist*); opposite the entrance, the tomb of Doge Andrea Dandolo (1343–54) who had the baptistery installed in the former ambulatory here; mosaic decoration (14th-century).

Y Cappella Zen (Zeno chapel). Impressive tomb (1505–21) of Cardinal Zeno; the sarcophagus, baldachin, statue of the cardinal and the other figures are all cast in bronze. On the altar is a Lombardesque *Madonna della Scarpa* (Madonna of the Shoe); according to legend, the Virgin presented a poor man with a shoe that turned to gold. In the vault, *Scenes from the Life of St Mark*; before the tomb was placed here, this chapel used to be the entrance hall to the basilica from the lagoon side.

Z ★ **Tesoro** (Treasury). Most of its precious possessions were captured during the sack of Constantinople in 1204; 11 niches contain 110 gold and silver reliquary caskets, studded with precious stones. The incense burner or coffer is in the shape of a Byzantine church; the so-called 'Chair of St Mark', a marble monolith of oriental origin (6th- to 8th-century); valuable Byzantine Gospel covers. Despite the fact that much of it was melted down in 1797 at the end of the Republic, the rich store of booty here is still very impressive.

Nuns in San Marco

23

Mosaic detail

In the gallery of the **Museo Marciano** (Museum of St Mark) are some very valuable works connected with the history of the basilica: tapestries, hangings, paintings, mosaic fragments and the original four gilded bronze horses which used to adorn the exterior of the Basilica. The gallery also provides a good close-up view of the *Apocalypse* mosaic (16th-century) and of the roof of the narthex; steps here lead along the walls as far as the transepts. It is worth studying the ★ **floor** of the basilica from up here: it was installed when San Marco was first built, and its slight undulations give a good impression of just how shaky the soil is beneath.

The Doge's Palace

★★★ Doge's Palace (Palazzo Ducale) ❾

Open: April to October daily 9am–7pm, November to March daily 9am–5pm; last admission 1½ hours before closing. A combined ticket includes the entrance to the Museo Correr, the Museo Vetrario in Murano and the Museo dei Merletti in Burano.

History of the building and its exterior

At the beginning of the 9th century the seat of the doges was shifted from the Rialto to San Marco; the first Doge's Palace burnt down in 976, the second in 1106, and the third had to make way for a new building before the visit by Barbarossa in 1177. Hardly anything remains of the four previous structures in today's building; the massive square pedestal on the left of the entrance, however, might once have been part of a corner tower.

Construction work on the present-day building began in 1340. Fresco painter Guariento was summoned in the year 1365, which means that the first section of the building facing the harbour basin was probably completed by then. Doge Michele Steno (1400–04) commissioned the intarsia ceiling in the Great Hall, and the magnificent windows facing the lagoon were added. On 30 July 1419 the Great Council *(Maggior Consiglio)* held its first session.

Pointed-arch windows and the bridge

The palace reflects (on a larger scale) the Venetian Gothic style used for residential buildings and shops: open arcades below, and a magnificent loggia above. The decoration – each arcade of the portico supports two arches of the loggia, ornamented with quatrefoil roundels – formed the basis for numerous variations throughout the city. The high wall is broken up by broad, pointed-arch windows (the two facing the bridge are still original); this three-level facade, which perfectly integrates structure, material and decoration, has been likened to an altar frontal in rich brocade. The balconied window in the middle was built by Jacobello and Pierpaolo Delle Masegne.

The second construction phase was the result of dilapidation: in 1424 the decision was made to demolish and rebuild the wing as far as the church in the style of the wing at the Molo which had already been completed. This was done by 1438, and architects Giovanni and Bartolomeo Bon, father and son, crowned their achievement with that supreme example of the Late Gothic style, the ★ **Porta della Carta** (1438–42), with its group showing Doge Foscari (1423–57) kneeling in front of the lion of St Mark. This graceful gateway filled in the last gap, and the new facade of the Doge's Palace was now complete after over a century of construction work. The 36 capitals (including those on the west facade) are superb examples of medieval carving. On the corners of the palace are some fine statues, including the *Drunkenness of Noah, Adam and Eve*, and the *Judgement of Solomon*. These three corners are crowned by three archangels: *Raphael*, representing trade, *Gabriel* (peace) and *Michael* (war). The Venetians' favourite attribute, *Justice*, crowns the balconied windows in the middle (Alessandro Vittoria, 1577–79). The marble ornamental crenellations on top of the facade are not just a unifying feature of the Doge's Palace; they are also repeated on the Procuratie, and extend around the square.

Adam and Eve

25

Once the exterior was complete, construction work carried on inside the building: the Arco Foscari, a groin-vaulted triumphal arch, was added as a continuation of the Porta della Carta and extended as far as the courtyard before its final completion under Doge Cristoforo Moro (1461–72); the sculptures of *Adam and Eve* are the work of Antonio Rizzo (the marble originals of 1476 are inside the palace; bronze copies in the courtyard).

The third phase of construction work was the result of a conflagration that destroyed the east wing next to the canal in 1483. Antonio Rizzo was commissioned to rebuild it, and he was followed by Pietro Lombardo in 1498 and then by Scarpagnino, both of whom carried out his

Courtyard of the Doge's Palace

plans. The Renaissance had arrived; the loggia with its pointed arches on the first floor is still Gothic, but the round arches everywhere else now set the trend. Rizzo's ★ **Scala dei Giganti**, the staircase used by the doges during coronation ceremonies, is named after Sansovino's colossal sculptures of Mars and Neptune. The exterior was completed around 1525, and now the interior needed to be decorated. Stonemasons from Tuscany, Lombardy and Venice had spent a century working on the building's Gothic wings and now shared the interior decoration with the greatest painters of the age. Bellini, Vivarini, Carpaccio, Titian, Veronese, Tintoretto and many others all decorated the Doge's Palace – and everything was lost in two fires (1574 and 1577). The stonemasons were more fortunate. A new building proposed by no less a person than Palladio was actually turned down; the Republic had long passed its zenith. The damage was repaired under the su-

26

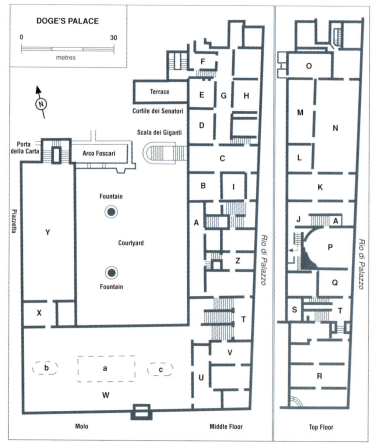

DOGE'S PALACE

0   30
metres

N

Porta della Carta

Arco Foscari

Scala dei Giganti

Cortile dei Senatori

Terrace

Fountain

Courtyard

Fountain

Piazzetta

Rio di Palazzo

Rio di Palazzo

Molo   Middle Floor   Top Floor

pervision of Antonio da Ponte and Bartolomeo Monopola. Towards the end of the 17th century the Doge's Palace finally received its present-day appearance, and the 18th century preserved it. The end of the Republic in 1797 and the decades that followed were difficult times as far as artistic activity was concerned; after Venice was incorporated into the Kingdom of Italy (1866) the new state ordered restoration work on the Doge's Palace. It was finally returned to the City of Venice in 1923. Venice now had its palazzo back again. With its two facades, the Doge's Palace is still the finest example of florid Gothic architecture in the city.

Interior

There is no single route for guided tours, because different sections of the building often need to be restored. Signs displayed in each of the rooms list their contents.

The Scala dei Giganti leads to a fine loggia with a good view of the courtyard. The two richly ornamented bronze well-heads date from 1554–59; the section of facade with the clock, between the stair and the entrance hall, the so-called Facciata dell'Orologio, is the work of Bartolomeo Monopola (1603–14). The small church of St Nicholas next door stands empty.

The small section of courtyard on the other side of the Scala dei Giganti is known as the Cortile dei Senatori (Senators' Courtyard), and is a fine Renaissance work by architects Spavento and Scarpagnino (1507). As in the Venetian house, the ground floor of the Doge's Palace was also used for various subsidiary purposes: the first floor contains assembly rooms and the doge's residence, and the upper storey contains the state rooms and council chambers.

A ★ **Scala d'Oro** (Golden Staircase). Designed in 1555 by Sansovino; named after the magnificent marble and gilded stucco decoration in the vaults.

The Scala D'Oro

Gilded stucco decoration

B Sala degli Scarlatti (Robing Room). This was where officials wearing scarlet togas would collect the doge. Intarsia ceiling in gold on blue background (1505); superb marble chimneypiece built by Antonio and Tullio Lombardo (1502).

C Sala dello Scudo (Shield Room). This is where the reigning doge's shield and weapons were kept; the armour belonging to the last doge, deposed in 1797, can still be seen. The maps date from 1540, and were restored along with the rest of the room in 1761.

D Sala Grimani. Wooden Lombardesque ceiling decorated with the coat-of-arms of Doge Grimani (1595–1605); sculpture frieze.

E Sala Erizzo. Lombardesque ceiling (early 16th-century); frieze with putti (17th-century); coat-of-arms of Doge Erizzo (1631–46) positioned above the marble chimneypiece.

F Sala degli Stucchi (Stucco Room). Fine stucco work with caryatids dating from reign of Doge Grimani (1595–1605); copy of Tintoretto's *Henry III of France*; from the window, a fine view of the apse of San Marco (11th-century).

G Sala dei Filosofi (Philosophers' Room). Doge Foscarini (1762–63) adorned the walls here with twelve philosophers from the cycle in the Old Library (*see page 15*); they were restored to their original place in 1929. Above the door leading to the staircase is the *St Christopher*, by Titian (1523–24).

H Doge's residence. Magnificent ceiling intarsias and marble chimneypieces; *Pietà* by Giovanni Bellini (1470); *The Damned in Purgatory* by Hieronymus Bosch; *Lion of St Mark* by Carpaccio (1516).

I Sala degli Scudieri (Palace Guardroom).

J Atrio Quadrato. Fine wooden ceiling (1560) with painting by Tintoretto.

K Sala delle Quattro Porte (Room of Four Doors). The four doors were designed by Palladio (1574–76); magnificent stucco ceiling with caryatids; ceiling frescoes by Tintoretto; wall frescoes depicting historic events; in front of the window, *Neptune Presenting Venice with the Fruits of the Sea* by Tiepolo (18th-century).

Sala dell'Anticollegio

L Sala dell'Anticollegio. Magnificent stucco and marble, and frescoes designed by Palladio (1576); paintings by the three contemporaries Tintoretto, Veronese and Bassano.

Sala del Collegio

M Sala del Collegio. Considered the finest room in the palace, because of the harmonious mix of decoration and fine art. Ceiling frescoes are by Veronese (1575); on the wall above the throne, the *Battle of Lepanto* by Veronese; wall paintings by Tintoretto.

N Sala del Senato. Another fine ceiling; the centrepiece is *Venice Exalted Among the Gods* by Tintoretto.

O Chiesetta. The doge's private chapel, also used by the senators; designed by Scamozzi (1593); a *Madonna* by Sansovino (1486–1570).

P Sala del Consiglio dei Dieci. The seat of the Council of Ten, founded in 1310.

Q Sala della Bussola (Compass Room). Antechamber to Council of Ten; on the right of the farther door, a *Bocca di Leone* (lion's mouth), a box in which secret denunciations were placed; paintings by the Veronese school; marble chimneypiece by Sansovino.

R Armeria (Armoury). The Council's private armoury, now a museum of ancient weapons.

S Sala degli Inquisitori (Inquisition Room). A council of three carried out interrogations here; a staircase connected it with the torture-chamber and the *piombi* (cells) beneath the roof. On the ceiling, *Return of the Prodigal Son* by Tintoretto.

T Scala dei Censori (Censors' Staircase).

U Andito del Maggior Consiglio (Corridor of the Great Council). On the left wall, works by Domenico Tintoretto, and opposite, by Palma Giovane.

V Sala della Quarantia Civil Vecchia (Old Courtroom). This is where the tribunal held its sessions for civil cases. The interior decoration is 17th-century. The adjoining room, the Sala del Guariento, contains the remains of a huge fresco (destroyed by fire) of the *Coronation of the Virgin* by Guariento, which he painted for the Great Council.

W ★★ **Sala del Maggior Consiglio** (Hall of the Great Council). This hall is where the parliament of patricians used to sit; sometimes as many as 1,600 of them. They ratified laws and elected the highest officials of the Republic. On 2 April 1849, during the Austrian occupation, *resistenza ad ogni costo* (resistance at all costs) was proclaimed here. The magnificent gold ceiling (1578–85) frames 15 frescoes. The centre panel (a) by Tintoretto: *Venice Surrounded by Gods Gives an Olive Branch to Doge Nicolò da Ponte* (1578–85); on the window side, by Palma Giovane (b) *Venice Welcoming the Conquered Nations Around Her Throne*; and the counterpart to this by Paolo Veronese (c) ★ *Venice Surrounded by Gods and Crowned by Victory*. The 21 wall paintings, depicting historical scenes, are by the workshops of Tintoretto and Veronese; on the window wall is Veronese's *Triumph of Doge Contarini after the Victory over Genoa at the Battle of Chioggia* (1379); Tintoretto's *Paradise* can be seen opposite it. Above the wall canvases is a long frieze showing the

Sala del Maggior Consiglio

29

On a conducted tour

first 76 doges, painted by Domenico and Jacopo Tintoretto; the portrait of Doge Marin Faliero, who was deposed and then executed in 1355, has been replaced by an inscription.

X Sala della Quarantia Civil Nuova (New Courtroom). A finely carved ceiling; no paintings.

Y ★★ **Sala dello Scrutinio**. This room was used to record the votes of the Great Council for the new doge. The frieze of doge portraits is continued in this room up to the end of the Republic in 1797. The ceiling and the long walls glorify Venetian victories. On the entrance wall is a magnificent *Last Judgement* by Palma il Giovane, and on the wall opposite a triumphal arch was erected in 1694 for Doge Morosini in honour of a victorious battle against the Turks; it contains allegorical paintings by Gregorio Lazzarini.

Z Sala della Quarantia Criminale. Nothing remains of this room apart from its gilt ceiling. The marble originals of *Adam and Eve* by Antonio Rizzo have now been placed here (bronze copies at the Arco Foscari, *see page 25*).

Sala dello Scrutinio

30

From the Scala dei Censori [T] several narrow passageways lead across the Ponte dei Sospiri (Bridge of Sighs, immortalised in Lord Byron's *Childe Harold*) to the *prigioni* (prisons); the way out passes the Sala dei Censori, the Avogaria (room used by a branch of the judiciary) and the Cancelleria (study). The dark dungeons known as the *pozzi* are also in this section of the building, and were reserved for the most dangerous criminals. The conducted tour, **Itinerari segreti** (English tour daily 10.30am, by telephone application, tel: 041 522 4951, or at the kiosk in the palace courtyard), shows visitors lesser known parts of the Doge's Palace by taking them through the maze of secret passageways and hidden chambers. It includes the seven prison cells beneath the lead roof, from one of which Casanova made his famous escape, as well as the torture chambers and the Doge's private apartments.

Column of San Teodoro

We now come back out into the open air; a few steps to the right are the **Colonne di San Marco e San Teodoro** (Columns of St Mark and St Theodore). These colossal granite monoliths were brought to Venice from the Orient in the 12th century and have stood on the Molo since 1172; between these two columns death sentences were passed, and many superstitious Venetians thus avoid walking through them. The lion of St Mark on the column on the palace side is of Oriental origin, and was once gilded. The statue of St Theodore on the other side (St Theodore was the patron saint of Venice before the relics of St Mark were acquired) is thought to be a Roman likeness of Mithradates, king of Pontus.

The lion of St Mark

Canal Grande

Route 2

Canal Grande (Piazzale Roma – Ferrovia – Rialto – Accademia – San Marco)

A trip along the 'S'-shaped Canal Grande (nearly 4km/2.5miles long), which divides the city into two halves, is an unforgettable experience; wealthy merchants and noble families positioned the facades of their houses to face the water. The city's optimal geographical situation – 4km (2.5 miles) from the mainland and 2km from the open sea – meant that strategic considerations never played a role, so warehouses, shops and private homes could be built in an open manner (*see page 8*).

The following is limited to a selection of the most important buildings to look out for during a water-bus or gondola trip along the Canal Grande, from the station to St Mark's Square.

San Simeone Piccolo

Opposite the station building, the large green dome and the portico of the church of **San Simeone Piccolo** ❿ catch the eye; built in1718–38, this was modelled on the Pantheon in Rome. Venetian legend has it that Canaletto was painting a *veduta* (view) here and felt there was something missing in his painting, so he 'invented' this mini-Pantheon; the Venetians are then supposed to have built the church based on the one in his picture – but it's probably just another tall story.

On the station side, just before the bridge, the facade of **Santa Maria degli Scalzi** ⓫ comes into view, with its mighty twin columns on two storeys and extravagant sculpture; the church is a fine example of Venetian neoclassicism, which is so often confused with baroque; it was designed by Giuseppe Sardi and completed in 1689 (*see page 62*). The bridge over the Canal Grande (one of only three) was built when Venice was connected to the rail-

Santa Maria degli Scalzi

way network in 1858; the former iron bridge was replaced by today's stone one in 1934.

Opposite the Riva di Biagio landing-stage is the church of **San Geremia** ⑫. Unusually, because of its position right at the junction of the Cannaregio Canal and the Canal Grande, this church was provided with two facades. Just after the church on the Cannaregio Canal is the **Palazzo Labia** (1750), a monumental neoclassical structure which was built by a wealthy family of merchants from Catalonia (*see page 62*).

The next landing-stage is named after the church beside it, **San Marcuola**; the brick facade only appears archaic – it was in fact constructed in the 18th century and never completed.

ROUTE 2

0   250
metres

Opposite is what used to be one of the finest Veneto-Byzantine buildings in the city until, sadly, it was unfeelingly restored in the 19th century, the **Fondaco dei Turchi** ⑬, which today houses the Museo di Storia Naturale (Natural History Museum, closed for renovation). The building dates back to the 13th century and used to belong to the dukes of Ferrara; the Republic used to 'borrow' the palace for state ceremonies. From 1621 to 1838 it was the warehouse of the Turkish merchants.

Fondaco dei Turchi

The brick building next door with the lion of St Mark on the wall used to house the *depositi del megio* (the granaries of the Republic) and was built in the 15th century. Opposite it is the ★ **Palazzo Vendramin-Calergi** ⑭, a massive Renaissance building by Mauro Coducci; the double-mullioned windows inside a large arch with a circle is a feature one frequently encounters in Venice, and was borrowed from Tuscany. Richard Wagner died in the Palazzo Vendramin on 13 February 1883 while a guest of the Duke of Chambord; the palazzo is the winter home of the Casino.

33

The next landing-stage is called San Stae (*see page 51*); next along this bank comes the **Ca' Pesaro** ⑮ built by Baldassare Longhena (1598–1682), whose monumental facades are a highly distinctive feature of the city.

The most interesting aspect of this building is the structural combination of sculpture decoration and columns – a recipe first used in Venice by Jacopo Sansovino when he built the Old Library (*see page 15*). Begun in 1676, the Ca' Pesaro was only completed by Antonio Gaspari at the beginning of the 18th century; today it is home to the Gallery of Modern Art and the Oriental Museum (*see page 51*).

Gondola on the Canal Grande

Water-bus in front of the Pescheria

The next landing-stage is named after Venice's most magnificent Gothic palace, the ★★ **Ca' d'Oro** ⑯. It was built between 1421 and 1440; its name is derived from its facade, which was formerly gilded. The first loggia floor (above the entrance on the waterfront) features the same decorative motifs as the external facade of the Doges' Palace, here exercising its influence a full 100 years later. The round arches in the middle of the ground floor presage the Renaissance. However magnificent the palace may look to us today, it was actually never completed; the left extension of the right wing was never built. The interior of the Ca' d'Oro palace has been restored and modernised and is a gallery showing paintings and sculpture (*see page 65*).

This fine Gothic jewel is followed by a neo-Gothic building, the **Pescheria** ⑰, a market hall built in 1907. On the same side, adjoining the ★ **Erberia** (wholesale market for fruit and vegetables), is the long arcaded **Fabbriche Nuove** ⑱; in 1513 a fire destroyed the entire Rialto quarter, and everything had to be rebuilt; this early example of Renaissance architecture is the work of Jacopo Sansovino (1552–55). Right at the centre of the 25 arches facing the water, take a look across at the 13th-century ★ **Ca' da Mosto** ⑲ on the other bank, a good example of the Veneto-Byzantine style. This was the birthplace of Alvise da Mosto (1432–88), discoverer of the Cape Verde Islands, and it later became a famous inn (the Leon Bianco).

The Canal Grande now begins its sharp curve to the right that leads to the Rialto Bridge; on the right before the bridge is the **Palazzo dei Camerlenghi** ⑳, which also had to be rebuilt after the fire of 1513. Directly opposite is the facade of the **Fondaco (Fontego) dei Tedeschi** ㉑, the former trading centre of the German merchants (*see page 42*). Today it houses the central Post Office. The

Fondaco dei Tedeschi

building was reconstructed in 1505 by Spavento and completed by Scarpagnino.

The Rialto Bridge (*see page 47*) was the only way of crossing the canal on foot until around 150 years ago; this is the very heart of Venice, the commercial centre where the Republic first began to flourish.

The **Palazzo Dolfin-Manin** ㉒ houses a modern-day commercial centre, the Banca d'Italia. Its white Renaissance facade, by Sansovino (1538), harmonises well with its blue awnings. Next door to it, in sharp contrast, is the **Palazzo Bembo** ㉓ with its Venetian Gothic facade.

Palazzo Dolfin-Manin

Among the row of seven different houses that now follow it's worth keeping an eye out for a narrow white house situated roughly at their centre; its windows have Moorish pointed arches.

On the same side now is another magnificent Byzantine building, the **Ca' Farsetti** ㉔ . The arches are no longer functional here (as on the Ca' da Mosto), but have become a decorative principle in their own right, covering the entire facade. Ca' Farsetti, built by Doge Enrico Dandolo, was heavily restored in the 19th century, and today houses the *municipio* (town hall).

35

Opposite, next to the San Silvestro landing-stage, stands the red **Palazzo Barzizza** ㉕, a rare example of a Byzantine house (12th to 13th-century); the remarkable reliefs on its facade date from the time it was built.

On the other side of the canal is the colossal facade of the **Palazzo Grimani** ㉖, a mighty Renaissance building by Michele Sanmicheli of Verona (early 16th-century), and next to it is the elegant Late Gothic loggia of the Palazzo Corner Contarini dei Cavalli (15th-century).

Palazzo Grimani

The other bank provides a good opportunity to study the different architectural styles: there is a colourful row of facades with Byzantine, Gothic and Renaissance arches. A particularly fine Late Gothic building is the ★ **Palazzo Barbarigo della Terrazza** ㉗, built around 1442, with its distinctive balconied terrace.

On the left of the Sant' Angelo landing-stage is the superb Early Renaissance ★ **Palazzo Corner-Spinelli** ㉘, built by Mauro Coducci at the end of the 15th century, with its rusticated ground floor and attractive balconies.

From the San Tomà landing-stage the four **Mocenigo Palazzi** ㉙ can be seen on the other side of the canal; the first one, a Renaissance building, has blue awnings which liven up its facade. Lord Byron used to live in the second one, which is rather wider and not quite as spectacular; the building has lions' heads along its full length.

At the bend in the Canal Grande here, the Rio di Ca' Foscari joins it from the right; on the other side of this junction is the complex making up the ★ **Ca' Foscari** ㉚, the University of Venice. It is one of the last Late Gothic

Ca'Rezzonico

Palazzo Grassi

Ponte dell'Accademia

structures in the city, with four storeys rather than the more usual three. Doge Foscari (1423–57) had the previous building demolished in 1452 and then rebuilt in its present form. It has fine tracery, and a frieze of putti bearing the Foscari arms.

The monumental neoclassical ★ **Ca' Rezzonico** ③, on the right of the landing-stage of the same name, was built by Baldassare Longhena in the middle of the 17th century. Its fine 18th-century interior decoration has been preserved (museum, *see page 56*).

Directly opposite is the **Palazzo Grassi** ㉜, designed by Giorgio Massari and considered the most remarkable example of 18th-century neoclassicism in the city. To the right of it is the 12th-century campanile of the former church of San Samuele; it is one of the oldest bell-towers in Venice.

On the right bank again we now pass a Late Gothic building, the 15th-century **Palazzo Loredan dell'Ambasciatore** ㉝, with Lombardesque Early Renaissance sculptures in its niches. The building was the Austrian embassy in the 18th century.

Anyone who looks across at the Ponte dell'Accademia (Academy Bridge) now will see the tall, narrow-shouldered facade of the former church of Santa Maria della Carità; at right-angles to it is the facade of the **Accademia delle Belle Arti** ㉞, built by Giorgio Massari (1760), which today houses one of the most important collections of paintings in Venice (*see page 61*).

Straight after the bridge, on the left bank of the canal, stands the ★ **Palazzo Cavalli-Franchetti** ㉟; its artistic 15th-century windows were inspired by those of the Doge's Palace.

On the other side now, the second building after the bridge is the long **Palazzo Contarini dal Zaffo** ㊱, one of the finest examples of late 15th-century Lombardesque architecture in Venice. On the same side, after the Rio San Vio, is the facade of the Palazzo Barbarigo, an architectural disaster for the Canal Grande and the city as a whole: its imitation mosaics, added in 1887, are disturbing.

Opposite is the **Palazzo Corner Ca' Grande** ㊲, the 'big house'; Sansovino designed it in 1532, after the previous building had been destroyed in a fire, and his innovations at the time included the rusticated ground floor and the triple-arched entrance. The upper storeys are lent emphasis by the use of Classical Orders (Ionic columns on the first floor, Corinthian on the second). Formerly the property of the Corner family, the building is today used by the provincial administration and the Prefecture.

On the right bank directly opposite is a one-storey flat-roofed building with a garden in front, the **Palazzo Venier dei Leoni** ㊳. Begun in 1749, today it houses the Peggy

Guggenheim Collection of Modern Art (*see page 61*); the Biennale has organised an international architectural competition for the building's completion.

On the same side there is another Early Renaissance jewel, the ★ **Palazzo Dario** ㊴. This Lombardesque building, with its polychromatic marble intarsias, was built in the late 15th century, possibly even by Pietro Lombardo himself. The actress Eleonora Duse (1859–1924) used to live here; she was born in Chioggia and the Venetians considered her one of their own. 'The Duse' ranks among the greatest actresses of all time.

On the other side of the canal once more, the 15th-century Palazzo Pisani-Gritti is easy to spot; today it is the celebrated Gritti Palace Hotel. John Ruskin stayed there in 1851, together with his wife Effie, before writing *The Stones of Venice*.

A side-canal now joins the Canal Grande, and the third house beyond it is the tiny and delightful ★ **Palazzo Contarini-Fasan** ㊵. It has wheel tracery on its balcony, and is traditionally called 'The House of Desdemona'.

The houses on the other side now gradually make way for the sales rooms of the great glassware manufacturers of Murano. Opposite, the only really striking-looking building among all the hotels is the **Ca' Giustinian** ㊶, a Late Gothic structure (c 1474), today housing the headquarters of the Venice Biennale and the administrative offices of the Venice Tourist Office.

Capitaneria del Porto

To the right of the San Marco-Calle Vallaresso landing-stage is the **Capitaneria del Porto** ㊷, a late-15th-century Lombardesque building. In the period 1756 to 1807 it was the headquarters of the Accademia di Pittura e di Scultura (chaired by Tiepolo), and today it is the Port Authority Office.

Distinctive prows

San Marco – La Fenice – Campo Sant'Angelo – Campo San Luca – Campo San Bartolomeo – San Giovanni Crisostomo – Santi Apostoli – Santa Maria dei Miracoli – Santi Giovanni e Paolo – Santa Maria Formosa

The facade of San Moisè

38

Leave the Piazza San Marco at its narrow end and head for the Calle dell'Ascensione; the Salizzada San Moisé leads to the church of the same name, and the Calle del Ridotto branches off in front of it. *Ridotto* formerly meant 'club' (redoubt), and from 1768 onwards so much gambling took place in this part of the city that the municipal authorities intervened in 1774 and closed down many establishments. Today this street contains the entrance to the Ca' Giustinian (*see page 37*), the headquarters of the Biennale and the administrative offices of the Venice Tourist Office.

The church of **San Moisè 🐵** dates back to the 8th century, and received its present appearance in 1688; its over-elaborate facade has several sculptures by Arrigo Merengo (the Austrian sculptor Heinrich Meyring), who also designed the high altar.

After the bridge comes the Calle Larga 22 Marzo, commemorating the day in 1848 when the Austrian occupiers were chased out of the city (for only one year, however). Crossing a canal, the street emerges at the square in front of the church of **Santa Maria del Giglio 🐵**, referred to by the Venetians as *Zobenigo* after the Jubanico family who founded the previous building on the site in the 9th century. The overladen baroque facade by Sardi (1678–81) was financed by the Barbaro family; the facade bears portraits of them and plans of Crete, Padua, Rome, Corfu, and so on, recording the victories of various members of their family in the service of the Republic. Beneath the organ in the sanctuary is a work by Tintoretto of the Evangelists. The *Madonna and Child with the Young St John* in the sacristy is actually half a Rubens – only the central section is genuine, the rest was painted by someone else.

Halfway back to San Moisè, the sign to Teatro La Fenice leads to the Campo San Fantin. The small church of **San Fantin 🐵** seems very inconspicuous at first, even though it was built by two famous architects, Scarpagnino and Sansovino, who began it in 1507 and completed it in 1564. Opposite the church stood the ★ **Gran Teatro La Fenice 🐵**. The famouse Fenice theatre, one of the finest opera houses in Italy was devoured by flames for the third time on the night of 31 January 1996. The theatre was burnt down in 1792 during its construction, then again in 1836; but it rose again from its ashes, like the mythical phoenix

Campo San Fantin

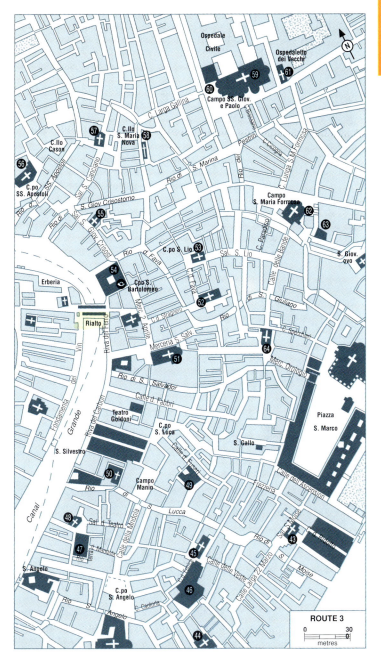

The leaning campanile

Palazzo Fortuny

Buying a ticket for an exhibition

– *fenice* in Italian – (*see page 88*). The theatre is to be rebuilt once again, and a special appeal has been launched to raise the estimated £200 million that will be needed for its restoration.

The small, two-storeyed palazzo with the triangular gable opposite the church is today known as the *Ateneo Veneto* and is a concert and conference centre; when it was built at the end of the 16th century it was the Scuola di San Girolamo, whose members used to give condemned prisoners moral support before their execution.

On the right-hand side of the opera house, the Calle della Fenice leads as far as a covered arcade and a bridge; at the next right fork the Calle Caotorta comes out into the **Campo Sant'Angelo (Anzolo)**. The leaning campanile of the former convent of Santo Stefano can be seen to the left; the plain wall along the canal here hides a superb Renaissance cloister that can be admired during office hours (the building is used by the financial administration). The campo is surrounded by Gothic facades; the opera composer Domenico Cimarosa used to live at No 3584 in the row of houses to the right.

Leave the campo via Calle della Mandola, a busy shopping street, and the first turn-off to the left, the Rio Terrà della Mandola, leads to the **Palazzo Fortuny ❹**, site of the permanent Fortuny Collection illustrating the artistic and scientific achievements of Mariano Fortuny y Madrazo (1871–1950), a Spanish-born 'Renaissance Man' whose name is linked with a type of precious, hand-woven and printed material he invented and designed in the early 20th century. The fabric is still made on the Giudecca and sold for high prices. The palazzo also holds temporary exhibitions. The 15th-century Gothic facade is impressive, as is the carefully preserved ★ **interior courtyard** with its fine old wooden staircase which seems not to belong to the building. (Closed until 2000 due to renovation, except for exhibitions, tel: 041 520 0995.)

One side of the building dominates the campo and the church of **San Benedetto (Beneto) ❹**, which contains Tiepolo's *San Francesco di Paola* (18th-century) in the first side-altar to the left.

The Salizzada del Teatro leads back to the Calle della Mandola; turn left into the Campo Manin with its mighty **monument** (1875) to Daniele Manin, who led the revolution against the Austrian occupation (1848–49). Follow the yellow sign suspended at the entrance of the narrow calle to the right of the monument, which points to the ★ **Scala del Bovolo ❹** . This is the beautiful external spiral staircase of the Palazzo Contarini, *bovolo* meaning *snail* in Venetian dialect, an astounding Lombardesque work dating from 1499. Cross this square now, and turn left at the modern building of the Cassa di Risparmio to

reach the campo containing the church of **San Luca**
The high altarpiece here of *The Virgin Appearing to St Luke* is by Paolo Veronese (16th-century).

Scala Contarini del Bovolo

Retrace your steps back to the Cassa Risparmio and turn left into the Campo San Luca, a popular rendezvous-point for the Venetians. A carved stone post with a flagpole marks the historic centre of Venice.

The Calle San Luca ends at the Calle dei Fabbri, the shortest route between San Marco and Rialto; it opens out on the left-hand side next to the Teatro Goldoni. Go over the bridge to the right (Ponte dell'Ovo), which leads to the church of **San Salvatore** , and the campo of the same name. A church stood on this site as long ago as the 7th century; the present version was built between 1507 and 1534 by architects Spavento, Tullio, Pietro Lombardo and also Sansovino. The lateral portal in the Lombardesque style facing the Merceria dates from that time; the facade was reworked by Sardi in 1663, who provided it with its sculptures.

The ★ **interior** is a superb example of Venetian High Renaissance architecture: clear lines, a generous three-aisled basilica on a cruciform ground-plan with three domes, and dynamic spatial rhythm achieved by the variously-distanced pillars along the nave. The most eye-catching works of art here are not necessarily the most valuable: there are two sculptures by Sansovino, *Carità* (Charity) and *Speranza* (Hope), next to the tomb of Doge Francesco Venier (between the second and third altar on the right-hand side); the third altar contains Titian's *Annunciation*, painted in 1566. The main altar contains a silver reredos, a masterpiece by Venetian silversmiths (1290); it underwent alteration in the 15th century and is revealed only between 3 and 15 August every year. This is compensated for by the fact that it is covered by a fine Titian *(Transfigurazione)*. The chapel on the left of the sanctuary contains Giovanni Bellini's *Cena in Emaus* (Supper at Emmaus). The crypt below the church can be viewed through a glass panel in the floor in front of the choir.

Cherub in San Salvatore

Leaving the church through the main door, the **Scuola Grande di San Teodoro** is very hard to miss; it was begun in 1579 and the facade was completed in 1648. St Theodore was Venice's patron saint before the city acquired the relics of St Mark; this *scuola (see page 11)* was devoted to merchants and arts and crafts, and the wares on sale on the ground floor continue the tradition.

From the Marzarieta 2 Aprile the route continues down the very first street to the right, the Calle degli Stagneri, and over a bridge to the church of **Santa Maria della Fava** , with its archaic-looking brick facade; the building actually dates from the 18th century. The interior is neo-classical and harmonious (Antonio Gaspari, 1711); the

Fondaco dei Tedeschi

combination of light and dark is convincing, and provides a fine setting for two remarkable paintings here: a Tiepolo in the first altar to the right and a Piazzetta in the second altar to the left (18th-century).

On the left-hand side of the church, the Calle della Fava branches off and ends up at the Campo San Lio; the church of the same name **53** is worth visiting for a look at its *James the Apostle* by Titian (on the left-hand wall of the second altar).

The continuation of the Salizzada San Lio (in the opposite direction from the church) leads to the Ponte Sant'Antonio; the ensuing shopping arcade then ends at the Campo San Bartolomeo, one of the busiest squares in the city, with its monument to Goldoni (1881). The **Fondaco (Fontego) dei Tedeschi 54**, the former German merchants' trading centre, today houses the central Post Office. The facade faces the Canal Grande, right next to the Rialto Bridge; the present Renaissance building by Giorgio Spavento and Sansovino (1505–8) has some fine arcades in its ★ **interior courtyard**; despite the four rows of arches the courtyard has a graceful, almost playful atmosphere about it.

Beyond the bridge, the Salizzada San Giovanni Crisostomo leads to the Renaissance church of the same name **55**, the last work of Mauro Coducci (1497–1504), who loved curved facades (*see San Zaccaria page 66* and *Ospedaletto page 45*). The spatial relationships within – a Greek cross ground-plan with a main dome and four smaller ones – have been somewhat disturbed by over-ornate decoration, though three works should definitely be mentioned: the chiaroscuro work over the high altar by Sebastiano del Piombo (1509–11) is very hard to see; Giovanni Bellini's *Saints Christopher, Jerome and Louis of Toulouse* (1513), one of his last works, is a lot easier to see and is in the first side-altar to the right; and directly opposite, on the left-hand wall, the marble altar by Tullio Lombardo (1500–2) has a classical bas-relief of the *Coronation of the Virgin*.

On the right of the church are two interconnecting courtyards known as *Corte del Milion*; Marco Polo (1259–1323) is said to have lived here.

The Salizzada San Giovanni Crisostomo now leads over a bridge where the Salizzada San Canciano branches off to the right. Across Campizello Corner, to the left, is a covered arcade with a bridge leading to the campo and church of **Santi Apostoli 56**, which underwent all kinds of aesthetically unsuccessful exterior alterations until the middle of the 18th century. The Cappella Corner (15th-century) by Mauro Coducci, an elegant Early Renaissance domed chapel, still survives; the altar has a *Communion of St Lucy* by Tiepolo (18th-century); and in the chapel

The clock of Santi Apostoli

to the right of the sanctuary there are several fragments of 11th-century Byzantine frescoes.

Covered arcades leading to Campo Santi Apostoli

From the square in front of the church the route now continues across the Campiello Cason and over the canal to the church of **San Canciano** ⑰, which was given its quiet pilastered facade by Antonio Gaspari in 1705. From here the bridge is only a few steps away to the left: boats used to leave for Murano from this part of the bank in former days. A few steps in the opposite direction and straight across the square is the church of ★ **Santa Maria dei Miracoli** ⑱. For the eyes of Venetians accustomed to brick facades (with the exception of San Marco), the Lombardesque style of this church, which was built by the Lombardo family of architects between 1481 and 1489, must have looked extremely odd. Fine polychrome marble inlay is the only form of decoration here, and Late Gothic formal geometry is reduced to a series of semicircles and right-angles: Tuscan architecture had finally arrived in Venice.

Santa Maria dei Miracoli

The interior of the church is surprisingly simple, with just one aisle, and the smooth walls are only broken up by the marble decoration. The vaulted and coffered ceiling, by Pier Maria Pennacchi and helpers (1528) contains 50 different portraits of prophets and patriarchs. The raised choir is particularly fine (the sacristy is below it), with superb marble inlay work on the triumphal arch, exquisite carving, and an eye-catching polychrome marble cross, typical of the Lombardesque style. The **Madonna** at the altar is supposed to work miracles, and was the original reason for the construction of this Renaissance jewel.

The Calle Larga Gallina leads around the apse and then to the right across the bridge to the ★★ **Campo Santi Giovanni e Paolo**, one of the most impressive-looking squares

Equestrian statue of Colleoni and Santi Giovanni e Paolo

The tomb of Giovanni Mocenigo

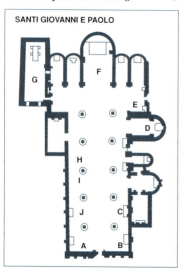

in the city: it contains the broad Gothic brick facade of the church of Santi Giovanni e Paolo; right next to it, at right angles, is the former Scuola Grande di San Marco with its cheerful semicircular facade, so typical of the Early Renaissance; and looking down rather gruffly at all this, the *condottiero* (commander of mercenaries), Bartolomeo Colleoni, whose huge **equestrian statue**★★ stands prominently in the square. He was a *condottiero* from Bergamo and a mercenary, and shortly before his death in 1475 he left a legacy to the Republic on condition that an equestrian monument was erected in his honour in the Piazza San Marco; in 1479 the Signoria ordered that it should be erected in front of the Scuola di San Marco instead. The Florentine sculptor Verrocchio received the commission for the statue, and it was finished after his death by Alessandro Leopardi, who also did the pedestal. Ever since its official unveiling in 1496, 'the Colleoni' has been considered one of the finest equestrian statues in the world.

The Dominican church of ★★ **Santi Giovanni e Paolo** ⑤⑨ (Monday to Saturday 7am–noon and 3–6pm, Sunday 3–6pm), familiar to Venetians as *San Zanipolo*, was started in 1234 and completed 200 years later in the Gothic style of mendicant order churches (*see page 84*). The upper section of the facade is harmonious; the lower section seems never to have been fully completed. The centre portal by Bartolomeo Bon (1464), however, is a masterpiece of Late Gothic sculpture; the bas-reliefs of the *Annunciation* flanking it are 13th-century Byzantine. The interior is divided by mighty columns of Istrian stone blocks, connected by the wooden tie-beams so typical of Venice, in three vaulted aisles; the main apse and the high altar are each flanked by two choir chapels – all five are closed off polygonally toward the southeast. San Zanipolo is the burial-place of no less than 25 doges.

SANTI GIOVANNI E PAOLO

A Tomb of Doge Giovanni Mocenigo, c 1500, by Tullio Lombardo.

B Tomb of Doge Pietro Mocenigo, completed in 1481, a masterpiece by Pietro Lombardo.

C Polyptych of St Vincent Ferrer, Dominican monk. These nine panels by Giovanni Bellini (1464) are a masterpiece of the Early Renaissance.

D Chapel of St Dominic, added between 1690 and 1716. Ceiling painting of the *Saint in Glory* by Giovanni Battista Piazzetta (1727).

E On the wall, *Christ Bearing the Cross* by Alvise Vivarini (late 15th-century). Stained glass of the window (late 15th-century) was made in Murano. Also includes *St Anthony* by Lorenzo Lotto (1542).

Ceiling in the chapel of St Dominic

F Choir. On the right-hand wall, tomb of Doge Michele Morosini (died 1382), contemporary Gothic; beyond it, of Leonardo Loredan (1572). On the left-hand wall, tomb of Doge Marco Corner (1365–68, the oldest in the church); behind it, tomb of Doge Andrea Vendramin (1476–78) by Tullio Lombardo (c 1492), the finest of the doge tombs.

G Chapel of the Rosary, added in 1582. Both rooms contain important works by Paolo Veronese (16th-century).

Sculptural detail

H Tomb of Doge Pasquale Malipiero (1457–1462) by Pietro Lombardo.

I Tomb of Doge Tommaso Mocenigo (1414–23), with an innovative baldachin carved out of stone, otherwise Gothic. This is a recurring motif throughout the city. Next to it (in line with the pillar) the tomb of Doge Niccolò Marcello (1473–74) by Pietro Lombardo, completed in 1481.

J Renaissance altar with good copy of a masterpiece by Titian, *St Peter Martyr* (1530).

At right-angles to the church facade stands the ★ **Scuola Grande di San Marco** ⑩ formerly a goldsmiths' and silk merchants' philanthropic confraternity, and today a hospital. The trompe l'oeil panels on the two-storeyed facade are very noticeable; the lions appear almost three-dimensional. The facade was designed by the Lombardo family of architects, and was finished by Mauro Codussi.

From here it is just a few steps to the monumental facade of the **Ospedaletto** (or Santa Maria del Riposo) ⑪ rebuilt by Baldassare Longhena in 1674. It is also possible to visit the *Sala della Musica* with its 18th-century frescoes and a small display of old musical instruments (Thursday to Saturday April to September 4–7pm, October to March 3–6pm).

The Calle dell'Ospedaletto leads to the Calle Lunga Santa Maria Formosa, at the end of which is the Campo Santa Maria Formosa. The church of **Santa Maria Formosa** ⏧ was, according to tradition, founded in the 7th century; it assumed its present-day form in 1492, and its interior is one of many to have been based on a Greek cross, like San Marco. Mauro Coducci put an Early Renaissance facade on the side facing the campo (1604); the facade facing the canal was added in 1542. To the right of the entrance on the canal side is the ★ **triptych** depicting *Scenes from the Life of the Virgin* by Bartolomeo Vivarini (1473); at the altar in the right transept, *St Barbara* by Palma il Vecchio (1509).

The route continues right round the church to reach the small street leading to the delightful ★ **Campiello Querini**; three canals meet here, and the various bridges afford magnificent views.

The **Palazzo Querini-Stampalia** ⏨, a 17th-century building, the residence of the patriarchs of Venice from 1807–50, contains a fine collection of paintings: works by Bellini, Palma Giovane, Palma Vecchio, Pietro Longhi, Tiepolo, and others, as well as the unusual series of 69 paintings by Gabriele Bella (mid-18th century) illustrating *Scene di vita pubblica veneziana* (Scenes of Public Life in Venice). The picture of the iced-over lagoon with Venetian skaters is especially captivating (Tuesday, Wednesday, Thursday and Sunday 10am–1pm and 3–6pm, Friday and Saturday 10am–1pm and 3–10pm).

Along the canal that passes to the side of the church of Santa Maria Formosa, the second bridge leads across to the **Calle del Paradiso**; a Gothic pointed arch made of marble, with a Madonna, can be seen between the houses at the entrance to the street. The houses here are ancient, some of them dating back as far as the 13th century, and this antiquity is what gives the Calle del Paradiso its special flair: both rows of houses have projecting first floors with charming medieval timberwork.

At the end of the Calle Paradiso, the Salizzada San Lio leads off leftwards to the Calle delle Bande, which goes right, crosses over a bridge and then suddenly reaches the back of the church of San Giuliano, known to the Venetians as **San Zulian** ⏩. The facade (on the right-hand side) is by Sansovino (1553–5); the church was commissioned by Tommaso Rangone, a doctor from Ravenna, and as well as his bronze statue (also by Sansovino) there are several inscriptions in Greek and Hebrew along the walls. The facade is rather cumbersome; obviously Sansovino wasn't all that inspired by the commission.

Near the back of the church, on the right, the Calle degli Specchieri begins; it was originally the street of mirror-makers (an offshoot of the city's glassmaking industry).

Route 4

The Rialto Bridge

Rialto – Campo San Polo – Ca' Pesaro – Campo San Giacomo dell'Orio – Campo dei Frari – Scuola Grande di San Rocco – Ca' Rezzonico – Campo San Barnaba

The ★ **Rialto** ⑥⑤ bridge (*see page 35*) crosses the Canal Grande at the heart of what used to be the busiest trading centre in the city. The names of the quays reflect it: the *Fondamenta del Vino* (wine) lies opposite the *del Carbon* (charcoal) and *del Ferro* (iron). Fruit and vegetables are still traded at the Rialto. Today's stone bridge (48m/157ft long), built in 1592, was preceded by wooden constructions; the two rows of shops on the bridge give it its distinctive, world-famous appearance.

Tomatoes for sale at the Rialto market

Directly to the right of the bridge, on the canal bank, stands the Palazzo dei Camerlenghi, a Renaissance building (1525–28, built after the fire of 1513). It used to be a financial administration building, and debtors were imprisoned behind the barred windows of its basement floor.

The bridge leads into the Ruga degli Orefici (Oresi), or Street of Goldsmiths, a name which points to just how wealthy this area was in former days; today this shopping street provides all manner of inexpensive souvenirs. The goldsmiths still have a church consecrated to their patron saint, too: **San Giacomo di Rialto** ⑥⑥, thought to be the oldest church in Venice, which is sadly closed to the public. It is the only one still to possess a Gothic entrance portico. The most distinctive feature of the facade is the Gothic 24-hour clock dating from 1410; it was restored in the 17th century along with the rest of the building. The Corinthian columns inside the church come from the building that previously stood on the site; the domed Greek-cross plan was faithfully preserved when the church was rebuilt.

San Giacomo di Rialto

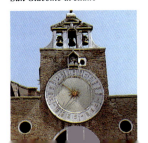

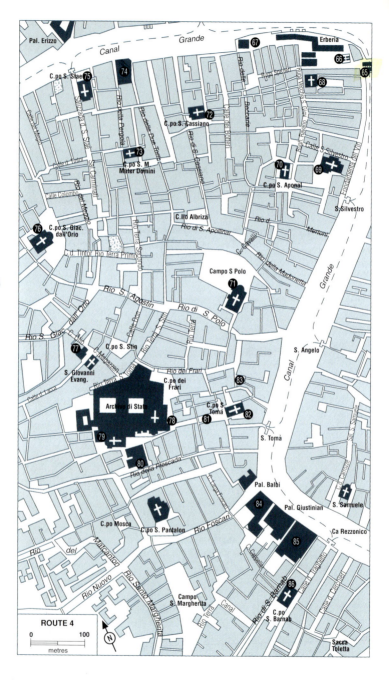

48

Pal. Erizzo

Canal Grande

Erberia

C.po S. Stae 75

74

67

66

65

68

C.po S. Cassiano 72

73

C.po S. M Mater Domini

70

69

C.po S. Aponal

S. Silvestro

C.po S. Giac. dall'Orio 76

C.llo Albrizzi

Rio di S. Apollinar

Rio d. Martori

Calle Colombo

C.d. Tintor Rio Terra Primo

Rio della Madonetta

Campo S Polo

71

Rio S. Agostin

Rio di S. Polo

Grande

Calle del Magazen

77

C.po S. Stin

S. Angelo

S. Giovanni Evang.

Rio del Frari

C.pa dei Frari

83

Archivio di Stato

78

81

C.po S Tomà 82

S. Tomà

79

80

Rio della Prescada

Pal. Balbi

84

Pal. Giustinian

S. Samuele

C.po Mosca

C.po S. Pantalon

Rio Foscari

85

Ca Rezzonico

Rio del Malcanton

Rio Nuovo

Rio Santo Margherita

Campo S. Margherita

86

C.po S. Barnab

Rio di S. Barnab

Canal

Sacca Toletta

ROUTE 4

0   100

metres

N

The Campo di Rialto in front of the church is enclosed by arcades built by Scarpagnino after the fire of 1513; the various laws of the Republic were proclaimed from the staircase opposite the church. The crouching figure supporting the flight of steps is the Gobbo di Rialto (Hunchback of Rialto), a figure of popular fun – like any other oligarchy, the Republic of Venice had a number of less well-off citizens who identified themselves rather cynically with the Gobbo. The architectural impression of this square as a whole is unfortunately marred by all the market stalls and barrows.

Canned drinks

The Ruga degli Orefici comes out into a small square with the market off to the right; after passing through the arcaded passageway to the bank of the Canal Grande, the Byzantine Ca' da Mosto (*see page 34*) comes into view on the other bank. The picturesque wholesale market for fruit and vegetables, known as the ★ **Erberia**, is held here each morning on the square next to the canal. The Calle delle Beccarie leads past the gracefully-styled Gothic market hall housing the **Pescheria** 🕖 to the Campo delle Beccarie; the Ruga degli Spezieri branches off it, and this short tour of the market area now ends at the small square in which it commenced.

The Erberia market

Towering between the houses in the Ruga Vecchia San Giovanni is the campanile of the church of **San Giovanni Elemosinario** 🕗, which was mentioned as early as 1051; it, too, had to be rebuilt after the 1513 fire, and it contains works by Titian's rival Pordenone, by Titian himself and by Domenico Tintoretto.

The Ruga Vecchia San Giovanni and its continuation, the Rughetta del Ravano, are the main arteries of this typical shopping quarter; the Rio Terrà San Silvestro now branches off to the right to the church of the same name. Though it dates back to the 9th century, the church of **San Silvestro** 🕘 was thoughtlessly restored during the 19th century; on the left wall is a Gothic polyptych in an elaborate 14th-century frame, and in the first side-altar to the right is *The Baptism of Christ* by Jacopo Tintoretto.

Exterior of San Apollinare

The shopping street now comes out into the small Campo Sant' Aponal, with its 11th-century deconsecrated church of **Sant' Apollinare (Aponal)** 🕙, which was given Gothic additions in the 15th century. At the centre of the church's brick facade, the soaring tendency of Gothic is well displayed by the early 14th-century *Crucifixion* below the window and the late 14th-century relief of the crucifix above it.

Opposite the church, the Calle de Mezo and the Calle Meloni lead to the bridge across the Rio della Madoneta; the ensuing arcade opens out into the ★★ **Campo San Polo**, one of the largest and most attractive squares in the city. Elaborate balls, parades and even bullfights were

Madonna and Child in San Polo

The campanile of San Polo

held here in former days; the poor of the city would buy cheap clothing at the various stalls here, beneath the proud facades of the palazzi surrounding the square.

★ **San Polo ❼** is entered through the Gothic portal in the right transept; the interior of this 9th-century church was restored in the 19th century, and it has a 'ship's keel' roof. On the left of the west door is a fine ★ *Last Supper* by Tintoretto (the one he did for San Marcuola is better, though). The painter Tiepolo also provided San Polo with some fine work: his famous ★ *Via Crucis* (Stations of the Cross) can be admired in the Oratory of the Crucifix. In the presbytery there are five large works by Palma il Giovane, which rather upstage the fine 14th-century crucifix with its yellow and gold tones.

Back in the campo it's worth taking a look at the campanile (1362), with its two fine Romanesque lions; it was a great help as a landmark in the old medieval city for those who had lost their way.

Between the Gothic and the baroque palazzi opposite the church, the Sotoportego dei Cavalli leads out of the campo; one bridge and two corners further ahead, the Calle de la Furatola leads over the bridge of the same name – where there is a fine panorama – before entering the arcade. The first turn-off, the Calle Stretta (Narrow Street), is easy to miss – it comes out in the Campiello Albrizzi with the palazzo of the same name, a typical 17th-century Venetian patrician's house that has had its interior preserved as a museum, exhibiting much fine furniture, stucco and paintings (open only for temporary exhibitions).

The Calle Albrizzi leads out of the campo. From the left, the Ramo Tamossi leads into the Carampane Passage, which leads across the Campiello of the same name and into the broad Calle dei Botteri, a shopping street that extends as far as the Canal Grande. Halfway there, a street branches off to the left to reach the church of **San Cassiano ❼**. The interior decoration of this building is not exactly modest; indeed, the altar paintings by Tintoretto are almost swamped by it. His eerie *Crucifixion* on the left wall is almost reminiscent of 19th-century realism. On the right wall is a *Descent into Limbo*. The last altar in the right side-aisle also contains a fine late medieval work which is unfortunately rather badly lit: *St John the Baptist Between Saints*.

Crossing the Rio di San Cassiano now, taking a left turn followed by a right turn, and then crossing a further bridge, we reach the Campo Santa Maria Mater Domini; in the background is the church of the same name, **Santa Maria Mater Domini ❼**. The sheer, almost Roman grace and purity of the facade of this High Renaissance building is particularly striking for Venice (*see page 85*). The church was consecrated in 1540, and its left transept contains an

important *Invention of the Cross* by Tintoretto as well as a fine 13th-century Byzantine bas-relief of the *Madonna in Prayer*.

The canal at Campo Santa Maria Mater Domini

The street continues past the church and reaches the rear of the ★ **Ca' Pesaro** ; yellow signs point the way to the Galleria d'Arte Moderna (closed for renovation until 2001) and to the Museo Orientale (open daily 9am–2pm except Monday). This imposing palazzo was built by Baldassare Longhena, Venice's leading 17th-century architect; he modelled it after the Old Library building on the Piazzetta. Since 1902 the Ca' Pesaro has housed a collection of modern art with a Venetian edge to it, but the gallery also possesses the largest collection of international modern art in Italy (including works by Utrillo, Rodin, Chagall, Vlaminck, Dufy, Rouault, Matisse, Max Ernst, Klee and Kandinsky). The Museo Orientale contains collections of Far Eastern art.

The Ca' Pesaro

Directly at the entrance to the museum, the narrow Calle di Ca' Pesaro crosses the canal and runs across the Rio di San Stae to the Campo and the church of **San Stae** , with its splendid facade facing the Canal Grande; it was built in 1709, and the architecture is neoclassical rather than baroque. The interior with its single aisle contains a superb collection of early 18th-century Venetian paintings – a real treasure-trove for art-lovers.

Commemorative plaque in San Stae

The Salizzada di San Stae continues into the Salizzada Carminati, from which the Ramo Carminati branches off to the right and leads across a bridge into the Calle del Colombo. At the end of this street on the left is the down-to-earth ★ Campo San Giacomo dell'Orio with its almost refreshing lack of ostentatious facades. The square is dominated by ★★ **San Giacomo dell'Orio** , a group consisting of a church and houses dating back to the 9th

century. It has been much altered over the centuries, but still has a strong archaic feel to it. To reach the main entrance one has to walk around the huge campanile (12th–13th century).

The church's interior is rather confusing, because the right transept is wider than the left one; if one stands beneath the crossing and follows the course of the 14th-century ★ **ship's keel roof**, the cruciform ground-plan becomes more obvious. In the south transept there is a fine Byzantine column of *verde antico*, and in the crossing is a free-standing ★ **pulpit** in the form of a chalice – its elegant marble intarsias are a real Renaissance rarity. The church was altered in the 16th century, and the impressive 14th-century crucifix in the sanctuary was brought here only in 1960.

On the left of the exit in the right transept is the entrance to the ★ **Sacrestia Nuova** (New Sacristy); the ceiling paintings are by Paolo Veronese (after 1570). Back in the church again, there is the Cappella del Sacramento, added in 1604; thanks to its harmonious Renaissance decoration, this 'church within a church' is actually quite self-contained. Another later addition was the chapel (1621–24) to the left of the main altar; the austerely-carved 14th-century statuette of the *Virgin annunciate* it contains was placed here only in 1972. The Old Sacristy, with its finely carved wood panelling, is entirely decorated with paintings by Palma Giovane (1575). San Giacomo dall'Orio is one of the finest churches in the city, and the square on which it stands is typical of *Venezia minore*.

52

Roughly in the middle of the row of facades facing the church, the Calle del Tintor leaves the Campo; shortly before the bridge (Ponte del Parrucchetta) it is worth taking a small detour off to the left for a glimpse of the **Campo San Boldo**: here a ruined campanile has been integrated into a residential block, and the scene is idyllic.

After the Ponte del Parrucchetta the Rio Terrà Primo leads to the Rio Terrà Secondo, which goes off to the right across a bridge into the Calle di Ca' Donà; the latter comes out in the Campo San Stin, which needs to be crossed diagonally. Just a few steps away now is the ★ **Scuola di San Giovanni Evangelista ⑦**. This *scuola (see page 11)* dates back to the year 1216. The first court has a beautiful marble screen and portal by Pietro Lombardi (1481): the facade on the left-hand side of the second court is 14th-century Gothic (the bas-relief showing brothers of the *scuola* kneeling in front of John the Evangelist is dated 1349), while the entrance to the *scuola*, with its double windows, is Renaissance (open: Monday only, 4–6pm).

The Calle del Caffettier and the Calle del Magazzen lead to the Rio Terrà S Tomà behind the Archivio di Stato; two bridges lead to the Campo dei Frari and to the church of ★★ **Santa Maria Gloriosa dei Frari** ⓻ (Monday to Saturday 10am–5pm, Sunday 3–5pm), one of the few Gothic churches in Venice (*see page 84*). The Franciscan mendicant order arrived in Venice in 1222, received the building land in 1250 and spent more than a century from 1340 onwards constructing today's church, the choir of which was consecrated in 1469.

Santa Maria Gloriosa

The facade and the architecture of the interior both reflect the Franciscan mendicant order's preference for simplicity, functionality and the absence of superfluous decoration: brick, rather than marble or gold. As a burial-place for families, however, the Frari church received a whole series of works of art – not all of them are successful, however.

A Tomb for Titian (c 1488–1576), erected in 1852.

B Sculpture of Bible translator Hieronymus, by Alessandro Vittoria (1560) in the style of Titian.

C ★**Marble choir screens** (1468–75) by Bartolomeo Bon, originally Late Gothic and completed in the Early Renaissance style by Pietro Lombardo; ★ **choir stalls** with elaborate carving done by Marco Cozzi from Vicenza (1468).

Statue detail in Titian's tomb

53

D Monument to General Jacopo Marcello, with the yellow-red-brown flag of St Mark; in front of the entrance to the sacristy, the fine Late Gothic tomb of Pacifico Bon (1437) who probably built the church.

E Sacristy. To the right of the entrance, a marble tabernacle attributed to Pietro Lombardo (1479); opposite, an elaborate baroque altar for reliquaries (1711); the triptych in the Cappella Pesaro (Pesaro chapel) is a masterpiece by Giovanni Bellini: ★ *Madonna and Child Between Saints* (1488).

F ★ **Polyptych** (1482) by Bartolomeo Vivarini, in its original frame.

G Cappella dei Fiorentini containing a masterpiece by Donatello in the altar niche, his wooden statue of ★ *St John the Baptist* (1451)

H Sanctuary, with Titian's incomparable ★★★ *Assumption*, which he painted between 1516 and 1518.

I Cappella dei Milanesi, containing the tomb of the man who founded opera, the former music director of St Mark's, Claudio Monteverdi (1643).

J ★ **Cappella Corner**; Late Gothic addition by the Corner family (from 1417). Monument to Federico Corner (Tuscan); stoup with statue of *St John*

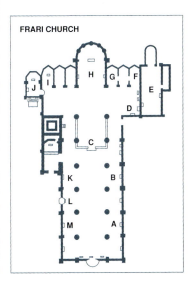

FRARI CHURCH

The Polyptych by Vivarini

San Rocco

the Baptist by Sansovino (1554); on the altar, *St Mark Enthroned* by Bartolomeo Vivarini (1474); 15th-century stained-glass windows.

K ★★ *Madonna di Ca' Pesaro* by Titian (1526), showing the Madonna and Child with saints before members of the Pesaro family.

L Tomb of Doge Giovanni Pesaro by Baldassare Longhena (1669), a bizarre and rather overladen baroque work.

M Mausoleum of Canova (1827), out of place here.

The church is only part of the complex as a whole; the Archivio di Stato (State Archives, containing the documents of the Republic until its end in 1797) are housed in the two cloisters adjoining it. The mighty campanile (the second highest in the city after San Marco) was completed in 1396.

The Campo San Rocco contains a fine group of Renaissance buildings, including the church of **San Rocco** , which, though begun in 1489, had its lines adapted to suit the Scuola Grande di San Rocco in the neoclassical style of the late 18th century (1765–71). The church contains some valuable works by Tintoretto in its sanctuary and organ loft.

The facade of the ★★ **Scuola Grande di San Rocco** ⓪ (December to February, Monday to Friday 10am–1pm, Saturday and Sunday 10am–4pm; March and November, daily 10am–4pm; April to October, daily 9am–5.30pm) is the work of two famous architects: Bartolomeo Bon (died 1529) from Bergamo designed the building and completed the ground floor with its playful, arched windows; Scarpagnino (died 1549) continued working on the building in 1535 and was responsible for adding the extravagant main facade.

The interior is world-famous for its paintings by Jacopo Tintoretto (1518–94). He was Venetian and, apart from a brief stay with his brother in Mantua when he was a very old man, he never left Venice. His artistic activity has left its traces everywhere in the city, but his pre-eminent work remains the cycle of over 50 paintings here in the Scuola San Rocco.

On the ground floor, the traditional reception room of the *scuole*, Tintoretto painted scenes from the New Testament: (from the left) *Annunciation*, *Adoration of the Magi*, *Flight into Egypt*, *Slaughter of the Innocents*, *Mary Magdalene*, *St Mary of Egypt*, *Circumcision* and the *Assumption*. The rather gloomy room inspired Tintoretto's clever use of light and colour.

The grand staircase by Scarpagnino (1544–46) has two huge paintings commemorating the end of the plague epidemics of 1576 and 1630, and it leads into the huge ★★ **Chapter House**. This vast room, with its many paintings, conveys a marvellous sense of unity and harmony; the floor and the altar with Tintoretto's *Glorification of St Roch* (1588) contrast with the rhythm of the ceiling frescoes on Old Testament themes. The wall frescoes are devoted to the New Testament.

Slaughter of the Innocents

55

Ceiling paintings

1   *Moses Striking Water from the Rock*
2   *The Fall of Man*
3   *God the Father Appearing to Moses*
4   *Crossing the Red Sea*
5   *The Rescue of Jonah*
6   *The Erection of the Bronze Serpent*
7   *The Vision of Ezekiel*
8   *Jacob's Ladder*
9   *The Sacrifice of Isaac*
10   *Manna Falling from Heaven*
11   *Elijah in the Wilderness*
12   *Elijah's Miracle of the Loaves*
13   *The Feast of the Passover*

The Fall of Man

Wall paintings

I   *St Roch*
II   *St Sebastian*
III   *Nativity*
IV   *Baptism of Christ*
V   *Resurrection*
VI   *Agony in the Garden*
VII   *Last Supper*
VIII *Miracle of the Loaves and Fishes*
IX   *Lazarus Raised From the Dead*
X   *Ascension*
XI   *Miracle of Christ at the Pool of Bethesda*

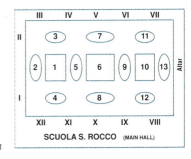

SCUOLA S. ROCCO   (MAIN HALL)

XII *Temptation of Christ* (with Tintoretto's self-portrait beneath it, 1573).

In the adjoining Sala d'Albergo, Tintoretto devoted his wall paintings to the Passion; on the ceiling can be seen his *St Roch in Glory* and on the far wall *The Crucifixion,* the most moving work of the whole cycle. Tintoretto worked from 1564–88 on these paintings, which are to Venice what the Sistine Chapel is to Rome.

Near the campanile of the Frari Church is a small street, the Calle Larga Prima, that leads behind the **Scuola dei Calegheri (Calzolai)** ❽❶ to the Campo San Tomà. The facade of this 15th-century 'Cobblers' Confraternity' contrasts with the opulence of San Rocco; the neoclassical church of **San Tomà** ❽❷ (1742) completes the scene.

A few steps away, left of the church and over the bridge of San Tomà, is the **Casa di Goldoni** ❽❸. This Gothic building was the birthplace of Venice's great writer of comedies, Carlo Goldoni (born 1707). The house is part museum part institute (closed for renovation).

Detail of the Casa di Goldoni

The route now runs parallel to the facade of San Tomà and off to the right to the Rio della Frescada; before reaching the bridge, turn right and cross the rio at the next bridge, which leads via a narrow lane to the Calle Larga Foscari. After the bridge over the Rio Foscari the interior courtyard of the **Ca' Foscari** ❽❹, the University of Venice (*see page 35*), comes into view.

Peaceful square near Ca' Foscari

Statue in Ca' Rezzonico

The street opens out into a picturesque little square, and the Calle dell Cappeller leads off it; after a right and then a left the street emerges at the Rio di San Barnaba and follows the left hand bank as far as the **Ca' Rezzonico** ❽❺, the Museo del Settecento Veneziano (Museum of the 18th century in Venice, closed for renovation until 2001).

This baroque building by Baldassare Longhena shows just how elegant the Venetian lifestyle was in the 18th century: stucco, marble, tapestries, ceramics, fine furniture, and valuable frescoes, including those by Tiepolo, father and son. An art gallery here contains works by Venetian genre painters Guardi and Longhi, and on the third floor is a reconstruction of an 18th-century apothecary's shop and a puppet theatre. The palazzo was once owned by Robert Browning's reprobate son, Pen, and his wealthy American heiress wife – it was while the poet was staying with them that he died of bronchitis in 1889 in the small apartment on the first floor.

The bridge over the Rio di San Barnaba is followed by the campo and the church of **San Barnaba** ❽❻, a neoclassical edifice dating from 1749, with a fine 14th-century campanile. The Calle del Traghetto on the right-hand side of the church leads to the Ca' Rezzonico landing-stage, connecting with San Marco and the Rialto.

Route 5

San Marco (S Zaccaria) – San Giorgio Maggiore –
Giudecca – Redentore – Zattere – Punta della Dogana
– Santa Maria della Salute – Collezione Guggenheim
– Accademia – Santo Stefano

San Giorgio Maggiore

Travel by water-bus from San Zaccaria (line 82) to the
Isola di San Giorgio Maggiore, and you disembark at the
parvis of the church of ★★ **San Giorgio Maggiore** ❸
(June to September, daily 9am–12.30pm and 2.30–6pm;
October to May, daily 10am–12.30pm and 3–5pm). Benedictine monks have been residing here since 982, and the
monastery has preserved an age-old cultural tradition as
the seat of the *Fondazione Cini*, with its artistic and scientific study centre. The few monks left here today live
a life of seclusion; they were deprived of their monastery
lands by Napoleon, and made a rare public appearance
in 1981 when US President Jimmy Carter was invited to
breakfast on San Giorgio as part of a trade summit. The
present-day complex is mostly Renaissance and is inex-
tricably linked with the architect Andrea Palladio
(1508–80); Baldassare Longhena (1598–1682) added the
double staircase and the library wing (closed to visitors).

For the church facade, Palladio resolved the problem
posed by the high nave and lower aisles here by inter-
secting classical temple fronts – one joining the side aisles
and the other, grander front superimposed upon it and covering the higher elevation of the nave. Construction work
began in 1566 and ended in 1610. The three-aisled ★ **interior** is the most spacious and light-filled in the city,
and its harmonious proportions make one forget the sheer
size of the building. Magnificent paintings here include:
first altar on the right, *Adoration of the Shepherds* by Bassano (1592); second altar, *Crucifix* (15th-century); third
altar, *Martyrdom of Saints Cosma and Damian* (Tintoretto
school); right transept, *Coronation of the Virgin* (Tintoretto
school); main altar, bronze group of the *Saviour on a Globe
Borne by the Evangelists* (Campagna, 1591–93); right-
hand wall, *Last Supper*, masterpiece by Tintoretto; left
wall, *Manna from Heaven* by Tintoretto. In the monks'
choir, the baroque stalls (1594–98) have fine wood inlay. Chapel to the left of the main altar, *Resurrection* (Tintoretto school); left transept, *St Stephen Martyr* (Tintoretto
school). Last altar on the left before entrance wall, *St Lucy*
by Bassano (1596). From the campanile (1791) there is
a superb view of the city (lift to the top). In the monastery
garden there is the Teatro Verde open-air theatre.

Before reboarding the water-bus it is worth stopping
to appreciate the panorama of San Marco across the water. At the next landing-stage, Zitelle, there is another

ROUTE 5
(1st Part)

0 ——— 50

metres

building by Palladio, the church of **Le Zitelle** ⑧⑧, a former hostel for young girls, and today an exhibition and congress centre. This facade of Palladio's has been much imitated (*see page 85*).

The walk along the **Giudecca** here affords superb views of the opposite side of the canal. House No 43 is the **Casa dei Tre Oci (Occhi)** ⑧⑨ (Three Eyes), an Art Nouveau structure influenced by Venetian Gothic. After the bridge comes the square in front of the ★★**Redentore** ⑨⓪ (1577–92), the first of Venice's two plague churches (closed for renovation until 2000). During the epidemic of 1576, in which Titian died, this building was commissioned by the Republic as a vow to God and designed by Palladio. The facade employs the same ingenious solution he used for San Giorgio Maggiore. The interior is not as bright, but the ★**apse** is a stroke of genius, lit from the dome above and from the choir, which stands behind a semicircle of Corinthian columns. The third chapels on the left and right contain paintings from the Tintoretto school; in the sacristy (entered via the choir) there is a fine *Madonna* by Alvise Vivarini (late 15th-century). On the third Saturday in July, the feast of the Redentore, a bridge of boats is constructed and a firework display is held in honour of the church's foundation.

Statue of Christ in the Redentore Church

58

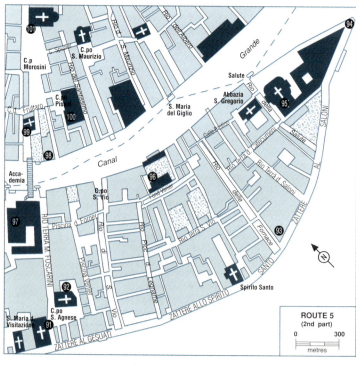

ROUTE 5
(2nd part)

0   300

metres

Santa Maria del Rosario

Reboard the water-bus which stops at Palanca before crossing over the Zattere. The facade of the church of **Santa Maria del Rosario o dei Gesuati** , despite its conventional neoclassicism, dominates all the others. The interior contains several magnificent 18th-century paintings, though. The statues between the side-altars go right round the room, and the bas-reliefs above them point the way towards the superb ceiling: Tiepolo's superb fresco (1737–39) is surrounded by monochrome contributions from his school. The ingenious use of colour, perspective and light here is typical of Tiepolo. The paintings in the side-altars maintain this high standard: in the first altar on the right, *Virgin with Three Saints* by Tiepolo (1740); second altar, *St Dominic* by Piazzetta (1743); third altar, *St Vincent Ferrer, Hyacinth and Ludovico Bertrando* by Piazzetta (1739); first altar on the left, *Pius V and Saints* by Ricci (1732–34); second altar, *The Virgin Mary* (neoclassical, 19th-century); third altar, *Crucifixion* by Tintoretto (1555–60). The elaborate high altar (18th-century) is encased in lapis lazuli and has precious marble columns. A few metres to the left of Santa Maria dei Gesuati is the less pompous facade of the little church of **Santa Maria della Visitazione o San Gerolamo dei Gesuati**, which is artistically a lot more important with its fine Lombardesque decoration (1494–1524).

On the Campo Sant'Agnese is the church of **Sant' Agnese** ②. Its exterior is Veneto-Byzantine (12th to 13th-century), with simple lines, rounded arches and brickwork. The fresco fragments inside once formed part of its decoration (13–14th-century; open: Sunday morning only).

One of the nicest walks in Venice is along the **Zattere**; from a distance the facades of San Giorgio Maggiore and the Redentore on the Giudecca opposite look as if they

59

Sant'Agnese

Santa Maria della Salute

The dome interior

actually are part of a painting. The **Magazzini del Sale** ⑨⑨ were the Republic's old salt warehouses; today they are open to visitors only when exhibitions are held.

Every ship that used the Canal Grande in the old days had to pass the **Punta della Dogana** ⑨⑨; at the extreme end of the promontory the little turret surmounted by a golden ball with a weathervane of Fortune supported by two telamones (designed by Falcone, late 17th-century) became a Venetian landmark. The view from here is always breathtaking.

The route continues along the city's old customs houses, and soon the church of **Santa Maria della Salute** ⑨⑨, Venice's second plague church, comes into view (Monday to Saturday 9am–noon and 3–5pm, Sunday 3–5pm). It was commissioned by the Republic as a vow to God during the epidemic of 1630, and of the 11 designs submitted the one by Baldassare Longhena was chosen; it was consecrated in 1687. The octagonal building, more a votive temple than a church, has a huge dome, and sculptured figures standing on volutes act as its buttresses. The columns and arches guide the visitor's eyes to the chapels and other parts of the building, almost as if it were a theatre. The high dome with its drum and large windows sheds a beautiful light on the interior with its circular aisle.

The first, second and third altars to the right of the entrance are masterpieces by Luca Giordano (late 17th-century); first altar to the left of the entrance, an *Annunciation* attributed to Liberi; second altar, *St Anthony and Venice* by Liberi (after 1652); third altar, *Descent of the Holy Spirit* by Titian (1555). Presbytery: colossal marble altar, designed by Longhena; *Madonna and Child* (Greco-Byzantine). Sacristy: over the altar, *St Mark Enthroned Between Saints Cosma and Damian, and Saints Roch and Sebastian* (1512); on the side walls, eight roundels (the Four Evangelists and Doctors of the Church) by Titian. Altar frontal: valuable 15th-century tapestry. To the right of the altar, a model of the *Salute* by Padovanino (17th-century). The wall opposite the entrance, *Marriage at Cana* by Tintoretto (1551). Beneath it, *St Sebastian* by Basaiti (early 16th-century), a fine Early Renaissance work. On the ceiling, *Cain and Abel, Sacrifice of Isaac,* and *David and Goliath*, all by Titian.

Before the bridge over the Rio della Salute there is a fine view of the apse of the former ★ **Abbazia di San Gregorio** (closed to the public). This Gothic building was designed by Antonio Cremonese (mid-15th-century); bricks were used for its simple exterior decoration. Over the bridge its facade can be admired: the portal, rose window and other windows have remained unaltered.

The Calle Bastion crosses the Rio delle Fornaci and, after a bend, broadens out into a campiello, to the right of which a bridge leads to the entrance of the **Collezione Peggy Guggenheim** ㉖ (daily except Tuesday 11am–6pm), with its many works of modern art (Chagall, Matisse, Klee, Picasso, etc).

From the Collezione Guggenheim

The Fondamenta Venier leads away from the gallery and along a pretty canal in the quarter of Dorsoduro; it then continues as a narrow street which comes out in the Campo San Vio. Across the Rio San Vio and through the Piscina Forner is the ★★ **Gallerie dell' Accademia** ㉗; entrance on the canal front (Tuesday to Saturday 9am–7pm, Sunday and Monday 9am–2pm, longer in summer). The 24 rooms cover all periods of Venetian painting from the 14th–18th century. The collections have been housed here in the former convent of Santa Maria della Carità since 1807, and many world-famous masterpieces are brilliantly displayed (Bellini, Piero della Francesca, Giorgione, Veronese, Titian, Tintoretto, Canaletto and Tiepolo, are just a few of the many artists represented).

The wooden **Ponte dell'Accademia** is an exact replica made in 1985 of the bridge that was built in 1932 to replace the old iron one of 1854. The view of the Canal Grande from here is world-famous; there is also a fine view of the Late Gothic facade of the **Palazzo Cavalli-Franchetti** ㉘, with its geometrically arranged arches. On the opposite bank is the deconsecrated church of **San Vidal** ㉙, which dates back to the 11th century. The facade was built in the Palladian style by Andrea Tirali in around 1700. There are valuable paintings inside: over the high altar is Carpaccio's *San Vitale*; the third altar on the right, *Archangel Raphael* by Piazzetta (18th-century); the first altar on the left, *Immaculate Conception* by Sebastiano Ricci (18th-century). The *Crucifixion* by Giulio Lama (early 18th-century) in the second altar on the left is also remarkable for its use of light.

Eating outdoors near the Ponte dell'Accademia

The enormous **Palazzo Pisani** ⑩⓪, which today houses the Conservatory of Music, is one of the largest private palaces in Venice. Begun in 1614, it has two interior courtyards divided by a huge open-arched loggia (closed to the public).

The Campo Francesco Morosini (commonly called the Campo Santo Stefano) was the scene of the city's last ever *Caccia al toro* (bullfight) in 1802. In this popular square is the church of ★ **Santo Stefano** ⑩①, with its magnificent Gothic portal by the Bartolomeo Bon workshop. The church dates back to the 13th century, but was later rebuilt in Gothic style. The interior was ready in 1374, and was given a ship's keel roof; the choir was added in the 15th century. The sacristy contains three fine works by Tintoretto: *The Last Supper*, *Washing of the Feet* and *Prayer in the Garden* (16th-century). The leaning campanile, built in 1544, is a familiar part of the city skyline.

Flower stall outside Santo Stefano

Route 6

Ferrovia – San Giobbe – Ghetto – Madonna dell'Orto – Abbazia della Misericordia – San Marziale – Ca' d'Oro

Towering next to the railway station is the facade of the **Santa Maria degli Scalzi 102**, a neoclassical building designed by Giuseppe Sardi. The church was begun in 1660 and consecrated in 1705. The interior is by Baldassare Longhena. During World War I this church lost its painted ceiling by Tiepolo (fragments can be seen in the Accademia, *see page 61*). The modern painting that replaced it, with the naïve bells at each corner, could happily have been left out. The interior is profusely decorated; the second chapel on the right and the third chapel on the left contain frescoes by Tiepolo.

The Lista di Spagna, the busy street in front of the station, leads to the Campo San Geremia with the church of the same name and also the pompous **Palazzo Labia 103**. The Labia family spent a fortune on their palazzo, and around the middle of the 18th century they employed some of the most famous painters around: Tiepolo, who was at the height of his powers, produced some superb

Palazzo Labia

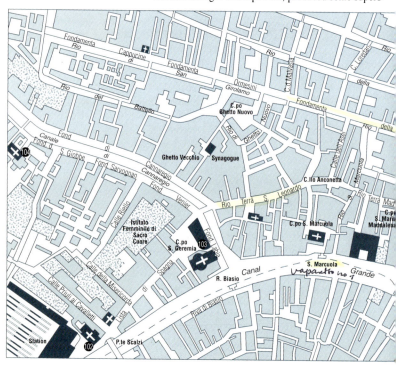

frescoes. The ★ **Salone** (ballroom) contains his *frescoes of Antony and Cleopatra*; the decoration of the entire room is magnificently harmonious. (Visits Wednesday to Friday 3pm and 4pm. Telephone in advance: 041 524 2812.)

Before the bridge over the Cannaregio Canal, the path on the left-hand side of the canal leads to **San Giobbe** ⑩⑫, an Early Renaissance church built by Pietro Lombardo (c 1470). The fine marble intarsia on the portal is continued in the interior. The area around the domed sanctuary is particularly elaborate; even the *Evangelists* in the pendentives are the work of Lombardo himself. In the second altars on the right and left respectively there is some fine marble, and the vault of the left one is also lined with majolica tiles and roundels: *Christ and the Evangelists*. The Cappella Contarini (entrance after the fourth altar on the right) still shows traces of the previous Gothic building by Antonio Gambello (mid-15th century); on the altar, *Presepio* (Nativity) by Gerolamo Savoldo (1540). The sacristy contains an *Annunciation* triptych by Antonio Vivarini (c 1445).

Cross the ★ **Ponte dei Tre Archi**, or three-arched bridge, over the canal here and walk back down the other side of the Cannaregio until signs appear pointing the way to the **Ghetto**. In the year 1527 the Republic gave the Jews – who were highly respected and an indispensable part of the city's economic life – permission to inhabit the part of the city formerly occupied by the iron foundry, and the area became known as *ghetto* (*gettare* in Italian means to cast metal). Synagogues, schools and eight-storey residential buildings have sprung up in this confined area.

The **Museo Comunità Ebraica** on the Campo di Ghetto Nuovo contains some valuable cultural artefacts (daily except Saturday and Jewish holidays 10am–7pm; October to May 10am–5pm). The synagogue tours also start from here (half past the hour 10.30am–4.30pm, daily except Friday, Saturday and Jewish

Washing near San Giobbe

Strada Nova
Shopping thoroughfare
no designer names.

Ponte dei Tre Archi

Museum sign in the Ghetto

ROUTE 6

0   300
metres

Madonna dell'Orto

Tintoretto's tomb

The oldest bridge in Venice

holidays; hours might vary, tel: 041 715359). The Schola Levantina has an elaborately carved pulpit; Baldassare Longhena designed the neoclassical Schola Spagnola.

A wrought-iron bridge leads from the Ghetto Nuovo to the Fondamenta Ormesini; the straight canals here with their continuous quays and views out to the lagoon are typical of the Cannaregio quarter of the city. The Calle della Malvasia connects with the next canal, the Rio della Sensa; next on the right comes the Campo dei Mori. The Venetians' general term for anything foreign to them was *moro* (Moorish), and on the house on the corner to the right there are three *Mori* statues set into the outside wall. The campo and church of ★★ **Madonna dell'Orto** **105** (Monday to Saturday 10am–5pm, Sunday 3–5pm) are named after a miraculous statue of the Madonna which was found in a nearby orchard (*orto*). Jacopo Tintoretto (1518–94), one of the greatest painters of all time, lies buried here. The brick facade is a fine example of Venetian Late Gothic (1462); the round arches at the centre already presage the Renaissance. The statues of the Apostles in the niches are by the Delle Masegne.

In the three-aisled interior there are some superb works by Tintoretto: in the choir are *The Last Judgement* (on the right) and *The Making of the Golden Calf* (left), both painted in 1546; in the fourth chapel of the left side-aisle, *St Agnes Raising Licinius* (1569); in the Cappella di San Mauro in the right side-aisle, *The Presentation of the Virgin in the Temple* (1552) – these last two are real masterpieces.

A modest slab in the chapel to the right of the choir marks Tintoretto's resting-place. The first side-altar to the right contains a *St John the Baptist* by Cima da Conegliano (1493); in the Cappella Valier, *Madonna and Child* by Giovanni Bellini (1480).

The route continues along the canal as far as the Sacca della Misericordia, and then turns right; before the bridge over the Rio della Sensa, the Fondamenta dell'Abbazia leads off to the left towards the campo, and then left again to the **Abbazia della Misericordia** **106**, built in the 15th century. The Late Gothic facade used to be that of the Scuola Vecchia della Misericordia, one of the city's six major confraternities (*see page 11*); unfortunately it is in urgent need of repair, as is the adjoining church of the former abbey dating from 1659.

Across the wooden bridge is the huge brick building designed by Jacopo Sansovino in 1532: the **Scuola Nuova della Misericordia** **107**, the new school. The exterior was never completed. Going left over the bridge opposite the school, you will see a tiny bridge without a parapet leading to a house. This is the oldest bridge in the city (13th-century), and is a typical Venetian construction with segmented arches and shallow steps.

On the path that runs beside the Rio della Misericordia stands the Palazzo Lezze, designed by Longhena in 1654. Passing the church of **San Marziale** , take the third bridge: the Calle dell'Aseo comes out into the Campiello dell'Anconetta with its neo-Gothic Teatro Italia, once a cinema. Over the Rio Terrà Maddalena is the Campo of the same name with the round 18th-century church. Stand in front of the portal and look right; there is a superb view across the roofs and chimneypots. The broad shopping street after the bridge is the Strada Nova, where there are stalls selling lots of enticing fruit and vegetables.

San Marziale

Until the end of the 17th century the Doge's Palace was the only building in Venice allowed to be called a *palazzo*. Other splendid mansions were called simply Casa, shortened to Ca', meaning house. The ★★ **Ca' d'Oro** is the finest Venetian Gothic palace in the city (*see page 34*). The lace-like facade, with its ogee windows, carved capitals, crowning pinnacles and bas-reliefs, was once covered in gold leaf – hence the name, House of Gold. Today the palace contains an important art gallery (daily 9am–2pm).

65

The interior has suffered many changes over the years and is barely recognisable as a 15th-century palace. The interior courtyard – where the stairway that used to adorn the exterior is preserved – is decorated with numerous works of art including the marble well-head by the man who built the palace, Bartolomeo Bon.

Stairway in the Ca' d'Oro

Baron Franchetti bequeathed his palace and collection to the state in 1916; he had collected valuable paintings, tapestries and sculpture from every epoch. His favourite piece was Mantegna's famous *St Sebastian* (c 1500), now on the first floor. Fifteenth-century Venetian bronzes and sculptures stand in the portico, which stretches the length of the palace as far as the loggia. Notable works are Tullio Lombardo's sculpted portrait of *The Young Couple* and the *Madonna and Child* marble lunette by Sansovino. The rooms to each side contain valuable paintings and smaller sculptures. From the end of the gallery there are views through the arches of the Grand Canal.

Fragments of frescoes by Titian and Giorgione from the Fondaco dei Tedeschi, and also by Pordenone from the monastery of Santo Stefano, can be admired in the hall on the second floor; the sculptures in the glass cases are by Bernini and Piazzetta.

The room to the left of the loggia contains a Bordone, a Van Dyck, a Titian and a Tintoretto; the rooms off to the right contain 16th-century Flemish works. The building also contains several panels by masters of the Tuscan school (15th-century). A real gem is the ★ **carved staircase** in the side-rooms off to the left.

Route 7

San Marco – Riva degli Schiavoni – Scuola di San Giorgio degli Schiavoni – San Francesco della Vigna – San Martino – Arsenale – Isola di San Pietro – Giardini Pubblici

Venice had particularly close ties with the Dalmatian coast, and the tendency in former days to refer to all the inhabitants of the coast as Slavs is reflected in the name of the landing-stage, Riva degli Schiavoni (Quay of the Slavs). First on this route are the **prigioni** (prisons) **110**, which were built in 1859 and are an essential part of any tour of the Doge's Palace (*see page 30*). Before the bridge stands a building worthy of its fine surroundings, the Palazzo Dandolo, a Late Gothic structure (15th-century), which has been a hotel since 1822. The second turn-off after the bridge, a low *sottoportego* (passage), leads on to the campo and church of ★★ **San Zaccaria** **111**, which together with its ex-convent makes up a huge complex. The Benedictine nuns of the former convent here were always given privileged treatment by the doges; they are said to have donated part of the convent orchard so that Piazza San Marco could be enlarged. The convent was vis-

San Zaccaria

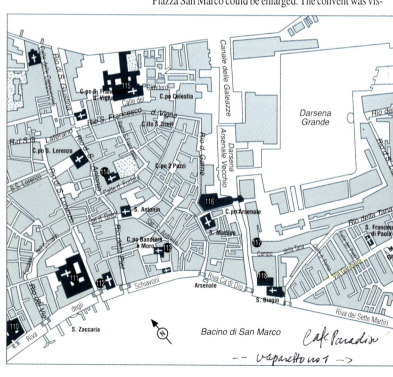

ited annually by the doge at Easter in gratitude for this gift and the ceremony also included the presentation to the doge of the ducal cap, or *cornu*.

The building dates back to the 9th century; its present appearance is the result of the alterations it underwent in the 15th and early 16th century, and the church also retains the 13th-century campanile from the previous building on the site, the Gothic *chiesa vecchia* (old church), dating from 1444–65. It was built by Antonio Gambello; he was also entrusted with the new building, which was continued after his death (1481) by Mauro Coducci. The imposing facade thus reflects the work of two very different architects: the two lowest storeys by Gambello are Late Gothic, while the rest of the facade is Early Renaissance, and was finished by Coducci in around 1504. The large round gables are unusual for Venice.

This mix of styles is continued inside the church in the ambulatory: round Renaissance arches crown Late Gothic pointed-arch arcades, the vault and the capitals recall Byzantine architecture, and the tomb slabs in the floor are Lombardesque. The sculptor Alessandro Vittoria (1524–1608) lies buried on the left-hand side of the ambulatory; he created the statue of the patron saint for the facade, and his graceful *St John the Baptist* can be admired next to the stoup near the entrance. He also designed the second altar to the right, which contains the relics of St Zacharias, as well as the tabernacle for the high altar.

Facade detail, San Zaccaria

Like many other churches in Venice, San Zaccaria was also packed with paintings during the 17th and 18th century; works more than worthy of attention here include the *Madonna Enthroned* by Bellini (1505) in the second side-altar on the left; in the altar of the chapel of St Athanasius (access to the right of the choir) there is an early Tintoretto, *The Birth of St John the Baptist*; the fine choir stalls for the former convent are by Marco Cozzi (1455–64), and the magnificent seats here

ROUTE 7

0   150

metres

nale di
a Nuova

C.po S/Pietro 119   **Isola di**
                    S. Pietro

Canale di S Pietro

d. Buga

di S.Anna

S.
Giuseppe

Rio di S Giuseppe

Giardini

Pubblici

Tomb with the figure of Christ, San Zaccaria

Interior of San Zaccaria

Santa Maria della Pietà

Ceiling painting by Tiepolo

were formerly reserved for the doge. The ★ **Chapel of St Tarasias** next door (Monday to Saturday 10am–noon and 4–6pm, Sunday 4–6pm) was the apse of the former church and contains fragments of flooring and frescoes as well as three magnificent Gothic altars by Ludovico da Forli (1443–44). The three paintings at the huge central altar are by Stefano Plebanus (1385). A stairway leads to the 9th-century crypt.

After the next bridge along the Riva degli Schiavoni there is an unpretentious-looking little church which possesses one of the most harmonious and successful interiors in the whole city: **Santa Maria della Pietà** ⑫. The church's conventional facade was designed by Giorgio Massari, and construction work began on the building in 1745; its elliptical ★ **interior** is highly original, however, and is reminiscent of a baroque one, though the style passed Venice by completely (*see page 85*). The interior decoration reflects the consistency of the architecture; the finely-worked gilt grilles are cleverly placed to their fullest advantage on the walls and balconies, and the muted pastels of the paintings on the ceiling and above the altar profit greatly from the gentle light they receive. The finest of the work here is by the two great 18th-century painters Tiepolo and Piazzetta: Tiepolo painted the ceiling himself, and Piazzetta the high altar (completed by his pupils after his death in 1754), above which there is another work by Tiepolo, the *Four Cardinal Virtues*. The effect of the whole is a masterpiece of architectural and artistic harmony, right down to the smallest details: even the carved baroque pulpit, with its gold and ivory tones, blends in superbly well. The organ here is famous: Vivaldi (died 1743) used to play it when the church belonged to the orphanage for girls where he taught music. The church is usually closed in winter, except for concerts in the evening.

The Calle Pietà runs past the right of the church; it then turns right and after the bridge comes out into the Campo Bandiera e Moro; on one side of this square is the Gothic Palazzo Gritti-Badoer (15th-century), and on the other the church of **San Giovanni in Bragora** . Its tripartite brick facade is Gothic in style; the church was built after the transition period and in style it presages the Early Renaissance.

The interior contains some wonderful paintings: at the high altar, a *Baptism of Christ* by Cima da Conegliano (1492–94); in the left choir chapel, a triptych of the *Madonna Enthroned* by Bartolomeo Vivarini (1478), and in the first side-chapel to the left, *Christ Resurrected* by Alvise Vivarini.

The Salizzada San Antonin leaves the campo on the right of the Gothic palazzo. On the right bank, just past the church of the same name stands the ★★ **Scuola di San Giorgio degli Schiavoni**  (April to October, Tuesday to Saturday 10am–12.30pm and 3–6.30pm, Sunday 9.30am–12.30pm; November to March, Tuesday to Saturday 10am–12.30pm and 3–6pm, Sunday 10am–12.30pm, closed Monday; tel: 041 522 8828). Today, this two-storey building (its facade was built in 1551) is well-known for its paintings by Vittore Carpaccio (1486–1525). Above the wooden panelling on the ground floor, his cycle relating to the lives of the three Dalmatian patron saints extends right the way round the room; the paintings were produced between 1507 and 1509. Here, Carpaccio has overcome the formality and stiffness of medieval painting; the vivacity and realism herald the Early Renaissance.

Keep left after the Calle Furlani, then go via the Campo delle Gatte, the Salizzada delle Gatte and the Ramo San Francesco della Vigna to reach the church of **San Francesco della Vigna** . This is where, according to Venetian legend, an angel addressed St Mark the Evangelist in a dream, saying *Pax tibi, Marce Evangelista meus* (Peace be with you, Mark, my Evangelist), the motto of the Republic (*see page 16*). A small church consecrated to St Mark stood on this site before the vineyard here was bequeathed to the Franciscan order for a convent. It was built by Sansovino in 1534; the facade is by Palladio.

The large interior (broad nave with side-chapels) contains the magnificent ★ **Cappella Giustiniani** (left of the high altar); it is decorated with precious marble from the Pietro Lombardo school (late 15th-century) – surprisingly, the picture of the founder (at the altar) shows an entirely different facade from the actual one by Palladio, in the Lombardesque style. The left transept provides access

Scuola di San Giorgio

69

San Francesca della Vigna

to the Cappella Santa; it contains Giovanni Bellini's *Madonna and Four Saints* (1507). There is also a charming *Madonna and Child Enthroned* by Antonio da Negroponte (c 1450) in the right transept. Bring along plenty of 200 lire coins to light up the paintings.

Leave the church through the portal of the right transept, turn to the left and take the Calle del Cimitero to the Campo della Celestia. This sleepy part of Venice seems to have remained unchanged for centuries. Cross the canal to the Campiello Santa Trinità, which branches off to the left from the Calle Donà; it, too, crosses a canal, and the first turn-off to the right, the Calle Magno, comes out in the Campo do Pozzi. Leave this square on the left-hand side in the direction of the Rio delle Gorne which runs along the wall of the Arsenal; along the bank of the canal is the church of **San Martino** which, according to legend, provided people driven from the mainland with a place of refuge as far back as the 6th century; Sansovino gave it its present-day look in 1540. The unusual feature of the ★ facade here is that Renaissance architectural forms have been achieved via the use of a very Gothic material: brick. There is no marble to be seen anywhere on this remarkable brick Renaissance facade.

Fishermen on the Rio delle Gorne

The entrance to the Arsenal

From San Martino, the main entrance to the ★ **Arsenal** ⑯ is just a few steps away. In former times this was one of the most strongly protected sections of the entire city; it was here that the Venetians protected their monopoly on shipbuilding, for their own and others' use, for trade as well as for war. The dockyard was first used in 1104; it grew into an installation covering 32 hectares (79 acres) and at the height of Venetian prosperity employed 16,000 workmen.

The great gateway in the form of a triumphal arch (1460, by Antonio Gambello) is the earliest example of Renaissance architecture in all Venice; the winged lion and the figure of St Justina, two favourite symbols of the Venetians, stand guard over it. *Justice* dates from the year 1578; the victory over the Turks at the battle of Lepanto in 1571 turned the gateway to the Arsenal into a memorial, and its decoration was extended with every further victory.

The colossal lion

The colossal lion sitting upright on the left was once part of a fountain at the Athenian port of Piraeus; it bears a runic inscription carved in 1040 by Scandinavian mercenaries fighting for Byzantium against Greek rebels. Francesco Morosini, who reigned as doge from 1688 to 1694, had it brought from Athens to Venice as booty – together with the other recumbent lion beside it.

The two towers at the entrance to the canal were built in 1574. Cross the Canale dell'Arsenale now and walk along the other bank as far as the Bacino (Basin) di San Marco. Halfway there the Campo della Tana bears off to the left; the **long building** ⑰ used to contain the *corderie* (rope-making section) of the Arsenal and is now used by the **Biennale** as an exhibition centre (*see page 89*).

On the corner of St Mark's Basin lies the **Museo Storico Navale** ⑱, the Naval History Museum, which also contains a collection of several thousand sea-shells (Monday to Friday 8.45am–1.30pm, Saturday 8.45am–1pm, closed Sunday and public holidays). The most spectacular of the exhibits here is undoubtedly the model of the *Bucintoro*, the name given to the ornate gala ship of the doge, with its 200 oarsmen, that was used for the Ascension festival of the marriage of Venice with the sea (*see page 89*). Shortly before the destruction of the last one of these ships, which was built in 1728, Admiral Paolucci had this model made (1824).

Next comes the little naval church of San Biagio (rebuilt in the 18th century) on the campo of the same name, and just after the first bridge is the Via Garibaldi – a filled-in canal which is wider than most of the other medieval streets in the city and thus looks rather like a pedestrian precinct. It passes through a lively residential area, and there are several fine views to be had down its side-streets. The church of **San Francesco di Paola** possesses a tasteful facade which will look very familiar: its unknown late-16th-century architect based it on Palladio's Zitelle on the Giudecca (*see page 58*); the two towers on either side of the triangular gable cannot have pleased him greatly, however, for he left them out. The interior has an elaborate ceiling with paintings from the Titian school; the restoration of the building as a whole, however, has not been all that successful.

The Via Garibaldi joins another canal with paths alongside it, the Rio di Sant'Ana; the bridge over the Canale di San Pietro affords a fine view of the various dockyard activity that is so characteristic of this quarter of the city. The island of **San Pietro**, a small village in itself, was the site of the cathedral of Venice from the 11th century until 1807, when the bishop's see was transferred to the Basilica of San Marco. For this reason, the church of **San Pietro di Castello** ⑲ is far larger than any village church, since it was the seat of the archbishops of Venice until 1807. The facade, with its pillared portico, is also very reminiscent of Palladio, and dates from 1596.

The interior, too, is very Palladian, and the church has undeniable similarities with the Redentore (*see page 58*). However, the interior decoration is much more elaborate. One of the most interesting features is the marble episcopal throne (*cattedra*) between the second and third side-altars on the right; it is said to have been used by St Peter at Antioch, and there are verses from the Koran and various Islamic motifs on the backrest.

Biennale sign

The model gala ship

71

San Pietro di Castello

On the way back, take the Calle Larga, the other bridge over the Canale di San Pietro; it provides a good general view of the church as a whole, including the gently inclining campanile designed by Mauro Coducci between 1482 and 1488.

The route then continues along the delightful little streets of the Campo di Ruga quarter of the city as far as the Rio di Sant'Ana and back to the Via Garibaldi; turn left at a small park and you will find yourself face-to-face with the statue of freedom fighter **Garibaldi** (1885), the hero of Italian unification. He is standing on a rock with a rather sleepy-looking lion of St Mark in the foreground; the whole is a work by the sculptor Augusto Benvenuti (1838–99).

The lion at Garibaldi's feet

72

Cafe paradiso

The park then leads on to the **Giardini Pubblici** (Public Gardens) proper, which were laid out on the orders of Napoleon. It is a place for recreation and it contains the exhibition pavilions for the Biennale (*see page 89*), the art exhibition held every two years.

At this point it is worth taking a few extra steps to see the church of **Sant' Isepo** (Venetian for *San Giuseppe*). Its Early Renaissance facade (1512), though in need of restoration, is still a fine piece of work. The perspective ceiling inside is attributed to Giovanni Antonio Torriglia; the imposing tombs of Doge Marino Grimani (1595–1605) and his wife were designed for the side walls by Scamozzi (c 1600); there are also two fine bronze reliefs by Girolamo Campagna.

From the Giardini, you can take a water-bus back from the landing-stage of the same name to the starting-point at San Marco.

Relaxing in the Giardini Pubblici

Route 8

Piazzale Roma – San Nicolò da Tolentino – Santa
Maria Maggiore – San Nicolò dei Mendicoli – San Se-
bastiano – Campo Santa Margherita – San Trovaso
– San Basilio – Sacca Fisola

From the Piazzale Roma a bridge leads over the Rio Nuovo
into the **Giardini Papadopoli** , a public park on the
site of a church and monastery. Cross the park to reach the
Campo dei Tolentini, which is named after its church, **San
Nicolò da Tolentino (I Tolentini)** 121. It was built by
Scamozzi between 1591 and 1602; its Corinthian portico,
based on the Pantheon in Rome, is by Andrea Tirali
(1706–14). The interior is conventional neoclassical, and
was filled with a wealth of stucco and paintings. On the
left wall of the high altar, the tomb of the great Venetian
admiral Francesco Morosini (died 1694) is noteworthy for
its colossal 'curtain' made of marble, a work by Filippo
Parodi, a pupil of Bernini.

Outside I Tolentini

On the left-hand side of the bank, walk past the church
and up to a bridge; after this, keep to the right and follow the other canal as far as a large wooden bridge; this
is a canal junction, and there are several bridges over the
various different canals that intersect here. After the large

Wooden bridge in Tre Ponti

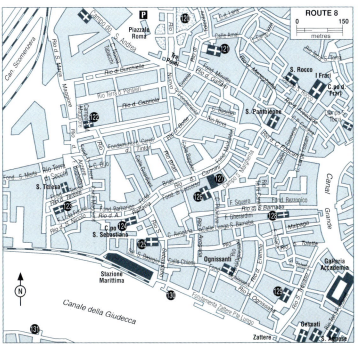

Café on the Rio Santa Maria Maggiore

One of the lion pillars

Exterior detail, San Sebastiano

wooden bridge go left along the side of the canal; this part of the city is named Tre Ponti because of all its bridges. Turn right on the Rio di Santa Maria Maggiore as far as the church of **Santa Maria Maggiore** 🅫; today the church and its convent are used as a prison.

Cross the bridge on the long side of the church and then take the first street on the right to reach the Fondamenta del Arzere; from there, the second bridge leads to the Fondamenta Teresa; turn left off it and across to the church of ★★ **San Nicolò dei Mendicoli** 🅫, which from the outside resembles a three-aisled basilica. This building dates back to the Early Middle Ages (7th century) and many believe that a pagan temple may once have stood on this site.

This part of the city to the extreme west enjoyed the privilege under the Republic of being allowed to elect its own representative; the people who lived here were known as the *Nicolotti* and their representative as the Doge dei Nicolotti. The pillars on the campo with the lions are a reminder of that time.

The structure of the church dates back to the 12th century; above the round window in the facade a Byzantine double-window can just be made out. The portico was reconstructed in the 15th century, using old material; the 14th-century nave assumed its present appearance only in 1580. The gilded wooden panelling, statues and paintings on the walls and ceilings all combine to form a fine Renaissance interior; from the high altar the pointed arches of the last two arcades can be seen. The apse was part of the original 12th-century building, and it contains some badly-preserved frescoes.

The 12th-century campanile seems particularly massive and cumbersome because it was never given a proper top; on the other side of it is the Rio di San Nicolò, and the second bridge along it leads across to the church of **Angelo Raffaele** 🅫. The church's organ loft is directly above its canal-side entrance; the parapet is decorated with some superb ★ **paintings** by Antonio Guardi (brother of the more famous Francesco) dating from 1750–53. Here he depicts the story of Tobias and the archangel Raphael. To the left is a *Last Supper* from the Veronese school.

Leave the church now via the side entrance, keep to the left and cross the campo. ★ **San Sebastiano** 🅫 is the burial-place of the great painter Paolo Veronese (1530–88). The ceiling here is worthy of the Doge's Palace: elaborately carved, it provides the perfect setting for paintings by Veronese (1556); he painted the large work above the high altar, *Madonna and Child with St Sebastian*, around 1560; the magnificent organ panels are also by him; the paintings on the walls of the altar date from 1565; Veronese himself lies beneath the organ to the right. The door beneath the organ loft leads to the sacristy, and Veronese proved just what a genius he was in 1555 when he painted its ceiling – after passing the test here on a small scale he was allowed to do the rest of the church too. The church portal faces a bridge; cross it then turn left along the canal bank, which makes a bend and then leads to the Campo dei Carmini with the Casa di Otello (Othello's House, closed to the public) at No 2615.

I Carmini (Santa Maria del Carmelo) **126** is the name of the former Carmelite church; its three-aisled basilica is separated by 24 pillars (14th-century). The ornate decoration of the interior, with its gilded wood panelling and paintings, dates mainly from the 17th century. In the second side-altar to the right is a *Presepio* (Nativity) by Cima da Conegliano (1509), and opposite it is a painting famous for its gentle landscape, *San Nicolò* by Lorenzo Lotto (1529). The ★ **side exit** next to it needs to be appreciated from outside the building: it is characteristically Gothic (14th-century), but contains Byzantine elements (11th to 13th-century).

The interior of I Carmini

Opposite is the ★ **Scuola Grande dei Carmini 127**, today a gallery (Monday to Saturday 9am–noon and 3–6pm; closed Sunday and public holidays). A staircase decorated with magnificent stucco leads into the *Salone*, with its nine fine ceiling paintings by Tiepolo from the years 1739–44, when he was at the height of his powers; light, space and colour all blend together perfectly in these works. As far as the other paintings here are concerned, special mention must be made of Piazzetta's incredibly expressive *Judith and Holofernes* (in the Room of the Archives, by the door).

75

Campo Santa Margherita

Like all the large squares in the city, the ★★ **Campo Santa Margherita** is very distinctive; medieval buildings, the seemingly sawn-off campanile at the other end, and a small market; house No 2931 is noteworthy for its use of the pointed *moresco* arch. The isolated building in the centre of the square was once a *scuola*; the worn relief of the *Virgin* with the brothers of the confraternity on the wall dates from 1501.

Take the Rio Terrà Canal and a bridge to reach the **Campo San Barnaba 128**, where the Calle Lunga San Barnaba begins; the first turning to the left, the Calle delle Turchette, connects with the Rio delle Eremite (Romite). This canal comes out in the Rio degli Ognissanti; follow its left-hand side as far as the church of **San Trovaso 129**, which dates back to the 11th century, though it received its present form from 1584 onwards.

Floating market near Campo San Barnaba

The left transept has a *Last Supper* by Tintoretto (1556) on its right-hand wall; the *Washing of the Feet* opposite is also attributed to him. There is another Tintoretto in the chapel to the left of the high altar: his *Temptation of*

Tintoretto painting
in San Trovaso

St Antony (1577). In the chapel to the right of the high altar is a Gothic painting, *St Chrysogonus on Horseback* by Michele Giambono (15th-century).

Before leaving the church via its right transept, where there is another exit, it is worth pausing and taking a look back inside: the elegant perspective altar with the Chapel of the Sacrament in the left transept (A. Vittoria, 16th-century) is most effective when seen from this distance.

From the canal-bank opposite the church, a *squero* can be seen at the corner of the two canals; it is one of the last remaining boat-building yards in Venice, where gondolas are repaired and built for the city's 400 or so full-time *gondolieri*.

The path beside the canal comes out at the landing-stage of Zattere on the Giudecca; the café terraces here to the south of Venice are a good place to get an early tan in the spring.

Water-bus

The next landing-stage, **San Basilio** ⓭⓪, is a short walk away; there is a good view of the skyline of Giudecca island along the way. It takes its name from Jewish settlers and was once a wealthy suburb of mansions and landscaped gardens. The massive ruined brick building is the Molino Stucky (Stucky Mill), a neo-Gothic flour mill built in 1895 and in operation until the 1950s.

San Basilio is close to one of the harbour entrances; at the landing-stage, take the water-bus to **Sacca Fisola** ⓭① and then walk the short distance to the campo. Geometrically laid-out new buildings, all of them very suburban indeed – this is another side of Venice altogether. At the landing-stage there are connections to San Marco and Piazzale Roma.

Excursions

North Lagoon

Line 52 runs from Fondamenta Nuove to San Michele and all landing-stages on Murano. Line 12 goes to Murano, Burano and Torcello. Line 14 connects San Zaccaria with Torcello and Burano via the Lido and Punta Sabbioni.

San Michele from the water

★ **San Michele**. This walled island is Venice's cemetery, and the oldest Renaissance church in the city was designed by Mauro Coducci. The vestibule is separated from the rest of the church by the monks' choir, which hides the interior with its ★ **coffered ceiling**. On the left just after you enter is the ★ **Cappella Emiliana** (16th-century). This hexagonal domed chapel, which Jacopo Sansovino completed between 1560 and 1562, is a masterpiece of Lombardesque marble architecture; the reliefs on the altar include an *Annunciation*, an *Adoration of the Magi* and an *Adoration of the Shepherds* by Antonio da Carona.

The church's characteristic campanile was completed in 1460; the portal with its pointed arch on the right displaying St Michael the dragon-slayer leads into the cloister, which in turn leads to the cemetery itself (opening hours: daily 7.30am–4pm). Those buried on this island include the poet Ezra Pound, the impresario Sergei Diaghilev and also his composer protégé Igor Stravinsky.

Restaurant in Murano

★★ **Murano**. On the Fondamenta dei Vetrai stands the 16th-century Lombardesque **Palazzo Contarini** ⓫. At

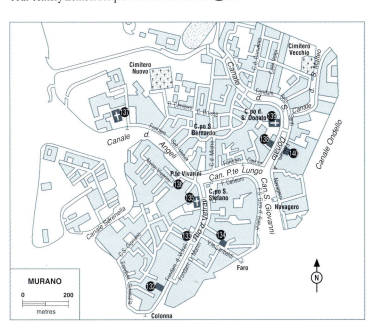

San Pietro Martire

Chiesa degli Angeli

Venetian Glass

Ponte Ballarin 133, proclamations were read next to the column with the symbolic lion; on the other side the Viale Garibaldi leads past the former **Teatro 134** to the lighthouse *(*Faro). Walking along the Fondamenta San Giovanni and Colleoni to the Campo Santo Stefano, there are fine views to be had of several magnificent facades; this world-famous island of glass-blowers was known for its prosperity and its generously proportioned palaces and gardens until its decline in the 19th century.

From the campo the bridge leads to the church of **San Pietro Martire 135**. The church is entered via its 16th-century Renaissance portal. On the right wall there are two works by Giovanni Bellini: *Madonna with Angels and Saints*, and *Madonna Enthroned*; on the left wall are *St Agatha in Prison* and *St Hieronymus in the Wilderness*, both by Paolo Veronese (16th-century). A short distance further on to the left, just before the bridge over the canal called Ponte Vivarini, lies the **Palazzo da Mula 136**. Though the facade is elaborate and Late Gothic, a delightful little ★ wall in the garden with Byzantine arches (12th to 13th-century) has survived (access via the courtyard when the glassworks are open).

The Lombardesque **Chiesa degli Angeli 137** can be seen from the canal bridge. The clear lines of its facade are convincing from a distance; close up, the building is in disrepair. After the bridge, the path along the canal leads around the promontory and to the ★ **Museo Vetrario di Murano 138** (April to October, Thursday to Tuesday 10am–5pm; November to March, Thursday to Tuesday 10am–4pm). The former bishop's palace (built 1698) contains over 400 items documenting the history of the famed Venetian glass industry from Antiquity to the present day.

Venetian glass: Why did the Venetians rely on glass-making, considering that they did not have the necessary raw material to hand? It seems that a gap in the market was discovered in the Middle Ages and actively turned into an absolute gold-mine. The famous Saracen glass-blowers in Syria (11th- to 12th-century) certainly sponsored trade with the Orient when Venice took up production. In 1291 the manufacturing installations were shifted to the island of Murano because of the danger of fire; from there, the whole of Europe was supplied with fine glassware and mirrors, until Bohemian glass finally dominated the market in the 18th century.

Being a glass-blower in Murano was considered a great honour, and entailed much responsibility: marriage into patrician families was quite normal, and revelation of trade secrets was forbidden under penalty of death. The craftsmen of Murano alone understood how to manufacture the thin, colourless glass and then give it its special elaborate designs and colours.

Apart from its glass, Murano's other claim to fame is the basilica of ★★ **SS Maria e Donato** ⓭, a superb Byzantine building dating from 1140. The shape of the arches clearly reveals the difference between the Byzantine and Romanesque styles. The simple clarity of line in the nave of this brick building is most impressive; in contrast, the apse, which faces the canal and was originally at the entrance to Murano from the lagoon, possesses a special elegance and beauty of its own: two tiers of arches are supported by thin marble columns, the upper arcade open, the lower one closed; the dog-tooth mouldings and carved and inlaid zigzag friezes surround the building like some archaic zip-fastener. The interior has a wooden ship's keel roof (early 15th-century). The mosaic in the apse dates from the time the church was originally built, as does the ★★ **mosaic pavement**, with its plant and animal motifs.

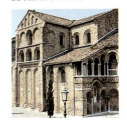

SS Maria e Donato

The path beside the canal now leads from the campo across the bridge and to the right, to the elegant **Palazzo Trevisan** ⓮, whose neoclassical facade is reminiscent of Palladio and still bears traces of earlier decoration. At the Navagero stop, line 52 connects with Venice via San Michele, or you can get off at Murano's Faro stop to take line 12 to Burano and Torcello.

Lace-making in Burano

★ **Burano**. This picturesque island village with its brightly-painted houses is the centre of the Venetian **lace industry**, another very useful source of income for the Venetians from the 16th century onwards. In the main square is the **Scuola dei Merletti** (Lace-making School), which still takes students and has an interesting museum (April to October, Wednesday to Monday 9am–5pm; November to March, Wednesday to Monday 9am–4pm). Burano's most famous son was the operatic composer Baldassare Galuppi (1703–85).

Torcello (founded in the 7th century) was once an important trading centre and had its own bishop. Today the

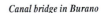

Canal bridge in Burano

79

The open timber roof of Santa Maria Assunta

Beach relaxation, Lido

Beach fun, Chioggia

island still trades in fruit and vegetables, and it also has two unique churches. ★★**Santa Maria Assunta**, the cathedral, was founded in the year 639 and consecrated in its present form in 1008. It is the oldest surviving building in the lagoon. Remains of the 7th-century baptistery have been discovered in front of its facade. To get an idea of just how grandiose the architecture is, the best thing to do is simply walk around the church: the south side is the only one with any windows, since no light ever comes from the north and making windows simply for decoration was still unheard of. The dignified interior (June to September, daily 10.30am–5.45pm; October toMay, 10am–12.15pm and 2–4.45pm) is remarkably spacious, with a superb marble pavement, the aisles separated by slender marble columns and spanned by an **open timber roof**. The greatest treasures are the 11th-century iconostasis (rood screen), consisting of four large marble panels elaborately carved with Late Byzantine designs, and the ★★**mosaics** in the presbytery which date back to the 7th century; the fine *Madonna* in the apse, however, is 13th-century. The dramatic *Last Judgement* mosaic on the western wall dates from 1190. The tall, square, detached campanile (11th- to 12th-century) is a striking landmark in the lagoon.

Archaeological finds can be examined in the **Museo dell'Estuario** (daily except Monday 10am–12.30pm and 2–4pm). Outside is a primitive stone seat known as Attila's Chair.

South Lagoon

From San Zaccaria, lines 82, 52, 14, 6, 1, and 4 (summer only) connect with the island of Lido – Santa Maria Elisabetta; from there bus 11 travels to the island of Pellestrina and then continues to Chioggia as water-bus line 11.

Lido. This island, with its fine, sandy beaches, villas, exclusive hotels and many sports facilities, is Venice's international summer health resort. The Film Festival takes place here annually from the end of August to the first week in September. The bus travels via Malamocco, the ancient harbour destroyed by a tidal wave around 1107, and then on to Alberoni on the southern tip of the island.

Pellestrina. This charming island with its fishing villages is ideal for quiet walks, and has its own shipbuilding industry near San Pietro in Volta. The mighty **murazzi** – a huge dyke over 4km (2.5 miles) long and 4.5m (14.8ft) high, the last great achievement of the Republic (completed 1751) – protects it from the open sea.

★ **Chioggia**. The geographical situation of this small town on two islands riddled with canals, forming a natural harbour at the southern end of the lagoon, could have had a positive influence on its development, but it never recovered from its destruction during the war with the

Genoese (1379–80). Today Chioggia is one of the main fishing ports on the Adriatic, though, and a huge market is held here every morning. In summer there are theatre performances and concerts. Goldoni immortalised the town with his *Barufe Chiozzote* (*Trouble in Chioggia*, 1760). The smaller island of **Sottomarina** is a beach resort.

At the Piazzetta Vigo landing-stage the main street, Corso del Popolo, begins beneath a shady series of arcades. Parallel to it on the left is the Canale Vena, a canal typical of the town. The Corso goes past the church of Sant'Andrea on the left (facade 1743) and then the long, one-storeyed *granaio* (granary), built in 1322, which survived the destruction of the town by the Genoese. On the canal behind is the famous fish market.

Fishermen in the harbour, Chioggia

At the next left-turn off the Corso is the **Chiesa della Trinità**, containing paintings from the Tintoretto and Veronese schools (16th-century). There is an elaborate coffered ceiling in the presbytery.

Two churches stand on the Campo del Duomo at the lower end of the Corso: ★ **San Martino** (1392), the small brick church with the square apse and octagonal drum, is a rather clumsy Gothic structure and was erected to commemorate the end of the war with Genoa. It contains a ★★ **polyptych** with 27 panels (dated 1349) illustrating the *Legend of St Martin*, attributed to Paolo Veneziano.

San Martino

The duomo of Chioggia was rebuilt in the neoclassical style by Baldassare Longhena after a fire in 1623, and construction work stopped in 1674 before the facade was completed. Inside the building, the unusual ★ **vaulted ceiling** of the baroque chapel to the right of the sanctuary with its stucco catches the eye.

On the way back to the landing-stage, a detour from the Corso to admire Chioggia's many fine Gothic and Renaissance facades is highly worthwhile.

Organ in the duomo

Art History

Opposite: the domes of
San Marco

Venice's early connection with Byzantium meant that it
also came into contact with Byzantine art: Byzantine artists
worked in Venice, the local inhabitants learned from them,
and several East Roman works of art found their way to
the city. This resulted in a development from the Early
Middle Ages onwards which made Venetian art distinctly
different from that of the rest of Europe.

Architectural elegance from the East

The domed church of San Marco, begun in 1063 (*see page
16*), was based on a Byzantine model, and its ground-plan
provided the inspiration for several of the churches in
the city right up until the 18th century.

Piazza San Marco

Characteristic of Byzantine structures is the high and
elegant round arch supported by slender columns with
richly-decorated capitals: typical examples are Fondaco
dei Turchi (*see page 33*), SS Maria e Donato on Murano,
and Santa Fosca on Torcello.

During the mid-12th century, when the powerful Romanesque rounded arch was dominating Central Europe,
Venice refused to adopt it – after all, it already had its elegant arches from the East. Romanesque in Venice can
only be traced to the architecture of certain campaniles.
The state church of San Marco did, however, receive a
Romanesque alteration on its facade (*see page 17*); after
all, the city's *nouveaux riches* merchants always wanted
the very latest of everything.

Venetian art has its contact with the Orient to thank
for its Arab inspiration: the Moresco (Moorish) arch became an enchanting window form. Beautifully sculpted
Moresco arches decorate the north portal of San Marco
as well as the entrance to its treasury. The East was also
the origin of the opulent mosaic decoration; the earliest
master mosaicists were probably Byzantine émigrés, and
some of their best work can be admired on Torcello (*see
page 79*).

The Gothic miracle

Gothic architecture originated in France in the 12th century, but it had lost much of its theological basis by the
time it reached the lagoon: the 14th-century Gothic icing that can be seen on San Marco today reveals that it was
simply borrowed as a means of decoration. The architecture of the Doge's Palace, however, shows how these
borrowed forms gradually blended into Venetian Gothic,
a decorative art that transformed the face of the city. Ogee
arches became a Venetian speciality – the Gothic severity from the north thus fell prey to Oriental fantasy and
secular curiosity.

*Interior courtyard,
the Doge's Palace*

*'Ship's keel' roof in
San Giacomo dell'Orio*

The miracle wrought by the advent of the Gothic style can be admired all over the city, and on the Doge's Palace as well as several facades along the Canal Grande in particular (*see page 31*). The soaring, cathedral-like aspect of Gothic is missing, though; the few Gothic churches Venice possesses are broad, rather stolid structures – for one thing the mendicant orders weren't too keen on the expense involved in building, and for another the land posed several foundation problems. The stone vaults that are the golden rule everywhere else are thus the exception in Venice (SS Giovanni e Paolo). Instead, Venetian ship's carpenters constructed wooden 'ship's keel' roofs – a real Venetian speciality (San Giacomo dell'Orio, San Polo, etc) – and also the wooden beams that were structurally necessary to strengthen the arcades and which actually contain iron chains (the Frari, Santo Stefano, etc).

Renaissance – the beginning of the end

The Lombardesque style (named after the place of origin of its main exponents) arrived in Venice in the late 15th century, and left behind several superb marble facades and intarsias (Palazzo Dario, *see page 37*). Very noticeable here are the playful semi-circles that were a particular favourite with the architect Mauro Coducci (San Zaccaria, Scuola di San Marco). He built the Palazzo Vendramin (*see page 33*) with its Tuscan Renaissance windows, and the Palazzo Corner-Spinelli, an Early Renaissance jewel.

Tuscan and Lombardesque influence: during the High Renaissance the spirit of Rome came to Venice in the shape of architect Jacopo Sansovino; his library building on the Piazzetta (16th-century; *see page 15*) completes the three main sources of inspiration in Venetian art: San Marco (Byzantium – East), the Doge's Palace (Gothic – North) and the Old Library (Renaissance – West).

The loggetta, Piazza San Marco

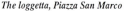

Very soon after Sansovino's death in 1570 a classicism, indeed almost a neoclassicism, emerged, but the use of pillars and arches for spatial effect on facades, borrowed from Antiquity, remained obligatory. But designers no longer wanted to rely on simple imitation, and this new architectural mood resulted in much that was vulgar: the city's buildings started growing extra pillars and whole storeys, and the skyline changed visibly. Buildings appeared which seem grafted on to the cityscape: Ca' Pesaro, Palazzo Labia, the Palazzo Grimani, Ca' Rezzonico, the Palazzo Grassi, Ca' Grande and the Palazzo Pisano are all variations on the same theme over a period of 200 years. The prolific ornamentation on the church of Santa Maria della Salute (consecrated 1687) by Baldassare Longhena is almost a symbol of this exhaustion of formal language; Venice, deprived of its earlier role as a world trading power, was putting up a facade to hide its loss of face.

Palazzo Labia

85

Palladio in Venice

The Renaissance architect Palladio (1508–80), from Vicenza, was unable to realise his monumental temple architecture in Venice, and so he altered his ideal of the Classical facade very constructively, in a geometrical manner: the churches of San Giorgio Maggiore, San Francesco della Vigna, Redentore and Le Zitelle are all masterpieces of harmony and clarity, as are the interior of San Giorgio Maggiore and the superb presbytery in the Redentore (*see page 58*).

Venetian baroque?

Several sacred and secular buildings appeared in Venice during the baroque era without actually being baroque structures; the style, which originated in Rome in around 1600 and took roughly a century to inspire countries north of the Alps, never caught on in Venice. Venice does not actually possess a single baroque building: several neoclassical facades overloaded with decoration are sometimes confused with the style, however (San Moisé, San Stae, Santa Maria del Giglio).

Facade of the Redentore

Painting

The connection with Byzantium and Orthodox severity meant that Venice hardly noticed the changes taking place in painting. The developments in Florence and Siena, and even the revolutionary work of Giotto in Padua, on the doorstep, were ignored for years. The construction of the new Doge's Palace changed all that, however: talented artists were brought into the city in the first half of the 15th century; they included Gentile da Fabriano from Umbria, and Pisanello, Paolo Uccello and Andrea del Castagno from Tuscany.

The main source of inspiration for Venetian painting was probably Andrea Mantegna (1431–1506), who married into the Bellini family of painters; he taught his father-in-law Jacopo (1400–71) and Jacopo's sons Gentile (1429–1507) and Giovanni (1430–1516), about the main achievements of the Renaissance: liberation from medieval formalism, and the introduction of perspective. The new realism then brought Antonello da Messina (1430–79) to Venice, and oil-painting came with him; he influenced the city's other great painting family, the Vivarini from Murano: Antonio (1415–76), Bartolomeo (1432–99) and Alvise (1446–1505). Both these families made Venetian painting so famous that even Albrecht Dürer was attracted to the lagoon in 1505 to learn from it.

The heirs to this legacy were the narrative painters Vittore Carpaccio (1486–1525) and Giorgione (1478–1510), who stood on the threshold of the triumphant 16th century, and were duly followed by the great master artists Titian (c 1488–1576), Tintoretto (1518–94) and Paolo Veronese (1528–88).

86

Painting had finally been freed from its medieval straitjacket, but each of these three artists used the space thus gained in a subjective way: Titian perfected the use of colour, and his work is distinctive for its humanity; Veronese, with his serene skies, is optimistic and worldly; and the expressive dramas of Tintoretto are full of searching questions: light, space and movement transcend the actual subjects of his work. He had a great effect on his most famous pupil, El Greco.

A Veronese in the Doge's Palace

After this high point of Venetian painting, Palma il Giovane (1544–1628) was still able to regard himself as the main exponent of the school until numerous imitators exploited the various painting methods. Originality finally returned only in the 18th century: painters Pietro Longhi (1702–85) and Francesco Guardi (1712–93) became chroniclers of Venetian life, while Antonio Canal (better known as Canaletto) became world-famous for his *vedute*, not only of his native city but of several others as well. The names Giovanni Battista Piazzetta (1682–1754) and Giovanni Battista Tiepolo (1696–1770) also belong at the latter end of the great era of Venetian painting; Piazzetta's pictures are more sombre and dramatic, while Tiepolo's luminous, poetic frescoes continue the tradition established by Paolo Veronese.

A work by Tiepolo

Sculpture

Byzantine severity dominated here, too, the only exception being the masterly sculpture for the middle portals of San Marco executed by Benedetto Antelami from Parma, when the basilica was being given its Romanesque facade (13th-century).

Renaissance sculpture

It was the large-scale project for the Doge's Palace in the 14th and 15th century that really got Venetian sculpture going, though: the two families of Bon and Delle Masegne worked together as combined architects and sculptors on the Doge's Palace/San Marco complex. The large window on the lagoon side of the Doge's Palace and the iconostasis in San Marco are by the Delle Masegne family, while the Ca' d'Oro and the Porta della Carta of the Doge's Palace are by the Bon family, and all are masterpieces of Gothic sculpture.

The early Renaissance (late 15th-century) was distinguished by the skills of the Lombardo family of architects: father Pietro (1435–1515) and his sons Tullio (c 1455–1532) and Antonio (c 1458–1516) built tombs and did much intarsia work for Venice's illustrious elite (SS Giovanni e Paolo, Santa Maria dei Miracoli, San Giobbe, sculptures on the choir screens in the Frari). The imposing equestrian statue of Colleoni on the Campo SS Giovanni e Paolo, which symbolised an epoch, was designed by Andrea Verrocchio (1436–88), and the marvellous statues of Adam and Eve on the Arco Foscari (interior courtyard of the Doge's Palace) are by Antonio Rizzo, who built the neighbouring Scala dei Giganti. Sculpture in Venice reached its high point with Mars and Neptune by the great Jacopo Sansovino (1486–1570), who also designed the Loggetta. He was assisted in his work on the Old Library and the Scala d'Oro (Doge's Palace) by Alessandro Vittoria (1524–1608).

The following period produced only undistinguished descendants of the great masters.

Colleoni

Music, Theatre and Festivals

Music

In 1527, the Flemish composer Adriaan Willaert (1480–1562) was appointed *maestro di cappella* of St Mark's. During his 35 years in the post Venice became the centre of western European music. He developed a style of polyphony in which two four-part choirs sang alternately, and this became one of the main characteristics of the Venetian school under his successors' Andrea Gabrieli (c 1510–86) and Giovanni Gabrieli (1557–1612).

*Plaque to Vivaldi,
Santa Maria della Pietà*

Another famous music director of St Mark's was Claudio Monteverdi (1567–1643), the founder of opera in its present form. By 1678 there were already seven opera houses (alongside 11 theatres that staged performances daily); among the more well-known exponents of Venetian opera were Francesco Cavalli (1602–76) and Marcantonio Cesti (1623–69). Venice's last great native composer was Antonio Vivaldi (1669–1741), who taught music at the girls' orphanage at Santa Maria della Pietà, and whose chamber music has survived to this day.

Theatre and literature

The style of improvised ensemble theatre known as Commèdia dell'Arte originated in Venice: the characters Arlecchino (Harlequin) and Brighella articulated popular sentiment in their never-ending struggle with Pantalone (Pantaloon), the merchant, and Balanzone, the doctor. The genre crystallised into a series of improvisations on stock situations until Carlo Goldoni (1707–93) created a new and more realistic form of Italian comedy. He held a mirror up to his country – and was exiled for his pains. Italy has not always been kind to its chroniclers: Casanova (1725–98) died in exile in Bohemia, and Lorenzo da Ponte (1749–1838), the famous Mozart librettist (*Don Giovanni*, *The Marriage of Figaro*) fled to America.

Concert poster

Events

The Teatro La Fenice has traditionally hosted opera, ballet and concerts from October to July. First built in 1792, it has staged various premières including Rossini's *Tancredi* (1813), Verdi's *Rigoletto* (1851) and *La Traviata* and Stravinsky's *The Rake's Progress* (1951). Since the theatre's destruction by fire in 1996, performances have been held at the PalaFenice on Tronchetto. For tickets and information contact the Cassa di Risparmio Bank in Campo San Luca, tel: 041 521 0161.

The Goldoni Theatre puts on works by Venice's most celebrated playwright, Carlo Goldoni, as well as classic plays in Italian, while the Teatro Al' Avogaria is a tiny theatre performing *Commedia dell'Arte* style plays.

Concerts of all kinds, from old music to contemporary, are held in the magnificent rooms of the city's churches and palazzos: the organ concerts in San Marco, San Giorgio Maggiore and Santa Maria della Pietà (where Vivaldi used to teach music) are very highly regarded. Chamber music, baroque and Venetian music are often performed at the Ateneo San Basso (Piazzetta dei Leoni), at the Scuola Grande di San Rocco in summer and at the Ateneo Veneto (Campo di San Fantin) in winter. At the Teatro Fondamente Nuove (near the church of the Gesuiti) you can listen to experimental and contemporary music.

Japanese Pavilion at the Biennale

The Biennale takes place every two years (from June to September/October). Although its official role is as an art exhibition (Giardini Pubblici since 1895), it also includes exhibitions of architecture and photography, as well as performances of theatre and music (Magazzini, Corderie, areas of the harbour and on the Giudecca).

During the Film Festival, but usually also in the months of July and August, movies (often in original language) are shown in the Cinema all'Aperto in Campo San Polo.

Festivals in Venice

89

The Carnival: This takes place 12 days before Ash Wednesday, and is the talk of the town; masked balls, a huge programme of events, and the whole city suddenly becomes a theatre.

Carnival mask

There are also several festivals that date from the city's days as a world sea-power:

Festa della Sensa (Ascension): On the Sunday after Ascension Day, celebrating the marriage of Venice with the sea.

Vogalonga: On a Sunday in May everything remotely seaworthy is hauled out for this huge rowing festival (*Vogalonga* means 'long row'). The route from the Giudecca Canal to Burano and back to San Marco is around 30km (19 miles) long.

Festa del Redentore: On the third weekend in July a bridge of boats is constructed across the Giudecca canal to the Redentore, the church built in gratitude for deliverance of the city from the plague of 1576. Boats are magnificently adorned and there is a fireworks display on the Saturday night.

Regata Storica: On the first Sunday in September this regatta, which features historical ships and costumes, is held in the Canal Grande.

Festa della Salute: In the second half of November a bridge of boats is constructed across the Canal Grande close to the Gritti Palace Hotel; on 21 November the procession leads from the church of Santa Maria delle Salute (built in thanksgiving for the city's escape from the plague of 1630) to San Marco and back.

Food and Drink

Venice is the most expensive city in Italy apart from Milan; the fare served by restaurants and *trattorie* here is usually not worth the price charged. Venetian cuisine can be superb; finding it, though – at a reasonable price – is a special art in itself.

A *trattoria* or *ristorante* usually serves three courses: hors d'oeuvres (hot or cold), a main dish with side dishes (vegetables or salad), for which an extra price is charged, and desert (cheese, fruit, or cake). To round off the meal, one can drink an espresso (*caffè*), with or without a cognac, or a *grappa*.

Meals in a *trattoria* can cost anything from 50,000 lire upwards. Bear in mind that the bill can grow considerably after the addition of *coperto* (cover charge) and *servizio* (service). The cover charge, however, includes bread. The oft-encountered *menu turistico* varies as much in price (22,000–45,000 lire) as it does in quality; cover charge, a drink and service are included.

The *rosticceria*, or self-service restaurant, has cheaper prices and the food is satisfactory; the menus do feature some Venetian dishes, too, and some lucky customers can have a quiet meal sitting down.

91

Pizza (which Italians accompany with a beer) is of course also available everywhere in Venice, in every possible variation. But do not expect central or southern Italian quality here, as there are no wood-burning ovens.

Pizza

Some bars in Venice offer all kinds of delicious foods that can be enjoyed on small plates accompanied by a glass of wine: every kind of seafood, served with steamed vegetables and *polenta*. Several *padroni* (bar-keepers) specialise in amazing sandwiches containing mushrooms, tuna, ham, egg, cheese and salad between layers of various types of bread.

Venetian cuisine

Most restaurants specialise in fish, and the range of specialities is vast, from *anguilla* (eel) to *zuppa di pesce* (fish soup). A *grigliata mista* (mixed seafood grill) is definitely worth investing in at least once. Connoisseurs adore the *risotto di pesce* (fish risotto) and will go out of their way to eat *granseola* (crab-meat with oil and lemon served in a shell). It takes a while to adjust to *bigoli in salsa* (black noodles) and *risotto nero* (black rice); the black colour comes from squid's ink. Not for the squeamish!

Seppie alla veneziana (squid with polenta) combined with *sarde in saor* (fried sardines marinated in vinegar, onions, raisins and pinenuts) is a classic Venetian dish. But fish is the main fare here; the only really popular meat dish in Venice is *fegato alla veneziana* (calf's liver with onion).

Fish for sale

Venetian wines

Wines served by the carafe or glass *(vino sfuso)* include Tokai or Soave (white) and Merlot and Cabernet (red). An additional *del Piave* on the label makes the latter two far nobler: the wine-growing area around the Piave river produces several full-bodied reds. Anyone keen on getting to know the wines of the Veneto well, should look for a *cantina* and do some detailed wine-tasting. Good whites – with fine variations in flavour – include the following: Pinot Bianco, Pinot Grigio, Sauvignon. Fruity reds include Raboso, Refosco and Marzemino.

Between six and eight in the evening, when the Venetians crowd the city's bars, the mixed drink known as *spritz* is consumed (the word dates back to the Austrian occupation): white wine with Campari or Aperol and a dash of soda. Another popular *aperitivo* is a glass of Prosecco (here called Prosecchino) or Cartizze, either plain or with a dash of strawberry, pineapple or blackcurrant cordial. The traditional, but less stylish *ombra* (plain white wine) still survives in the San Marco neighbourhood.

al mascarone

Cafe paradiso

Restaurant at the Rialto Bridge

Famous eating and drinking establishments

Danieli Terrace, Riva degli Schiavoni, 4196 Castello. A top-class restaurant with an enchanting view of the lagoon; **Gritti**, Campo Santa Maria del Giglio, 2467 San Marco. Old recipes from the splendid days of the doges; **Da Fiore**, Calle del Scaleter, 2202/A San Polo. A very popular and excellent fish restaurant. **Locanda Montin**, Fondamenta della Eremite, 1147 Dorsoduro. **Harry's Bar**, Calle Vallaresso, 1323 San Marco. The most famous bar in Venice: Hemingway's ghost appears on moveable feast days; **Caffè Florian**, Piazza San Marco. The oldest coffee house in all Italy, once frequented by Goethe, Mark Twain, Thomas Mann and Ernest Hemingway.

Shopping

Venetian craftsmanship continues to flourish. You don't have to look far to find fascinating specialist shops and local artisans at work in their ateliers. Look out for beautifully crafted Venetian masks, marbled paper, Murano glass, handmade picture frames, lace, linen and jewellery.

Murano glass

The arcades of Piazza San Marco shelter luxury jewellers, hand-embroidered linen and lace, and priceless pieces of glass. The Mercerie, which links Piazza San Marco with the Rialto, is still a busy shopping thoroughfare. Best buys in the area are silk ties, soft leather wallets, lamb's-wool and angora sweaters. In the Ruga degli Orefici, street of the goldsmiths, jewellers have hung out for centuries.

Arts and Crafts

To see authentic Venetian crafts visit **Veneziartigiana** at 412–413 Calle Larga San Marco, just north of the Basilica. This is a fine old apothecary shop converted into a showroom for crafts designed in glass, silver, bronze, china, lace and gold. **Jesurum** on Piazza San Marco and Merceria del Capitello 4857, is a long-established name in lace and linen, while **Trois** on Campo San Maurizio, sells fine silks and exotic hand-printed fabrics, including Fortuny-inspired designs. Glass has been made in Venice for centuries, and the items for sale range from tiny glass insects to vast chandeliers. The best choice is found on the glass-making island of Murano where there are many shops and showrooms. Some of the manufacturers also have outlets in Venice, on or close to Piazza San Marco. The city has a splendid choice of masks, and some of the most eye-catching can be found at **Tragicomica**, Campiello dei Meloni, San Polo 1414, **Laboratorio Artigiano Maschere**, Barbaria delle Tole, Castello 6657, **Mondo Novo** at Rio Terrà Canal, Santa Margherita, Dorsoduro 3063, and **Ca' Macana** at Calle de le Botteghe, San Barnaba, Dorsoduro 3172. For hand-printed paper with marble designs and other fine stationery, visit **Legatoria Piazzesi**, Campiello della Feltrina, San Marco 2511c. You can see the antique woodblocks which are still used to make the paper by the traditional *carta varese* method.

93

Burano lace

Fashion

The Calle Larga XXII Marzo and the streets between here and Piazza San Marco are the smartest shopping addresses in town. The Salizzada San Moisè boasts big names in shoes, bags and fashions. Slightly more off-beat and fun is the street called **Frezzeria** running north of the Salizzada San Moisé, while **Fiorella** in the Campo Santo Stefano is renowned for the most outlandish fashions.

Venetian sandals

strada nova

Getting There

By plane

British Airways and Alitalia operate direct flights from London Heathrow airport. Many of the charter flights from the UK operate to Treviso, 30km (20 miles) north of Venice. There are no direct flights to Venice from the US.

Marco Polo airport is 9km (5½miles) north of Venice in Tessera near Mestre (*see Map, page 6,* tel: 041 260 9260). To get to the city takes 30 minutes by a bus that runs as far as the Piazzale Roma (buy tickets from the ATVO office in the arrival area or on board the bus when office is closed), or 45 minutes by the more romantic *motoscafo* (motor-boat) to San Marco, via Murano and the Lido. Treviso airport is connected to Venice by public buses and a frequent train service.

By rail

Venice is connected with the international rail network by the main station of Santa Lucia. Arriving by train you have the advantage of an information office within the station, more porters available and a wide choice of water transport below the station.

The railway station

95

By car

Arriving by car is best avoided. Garaging costs are high and space at Piazzale Roma for most of the year is non-existent. This means parking outside Venice, either at Tronchetto (a parking island) or Fusina, found at the mouth of the Brenta Canal.

Visitors from the north will approach either from Austria or Switzerland. The main traffic routes are as follows:
- Innsbruck over the Brenner Pass, Bolzano, Trient, Verona, Padua, Venice. Always on the motorway.
- Innsbruck over the Brenner Pass, Bolzano, Trient, Bassano, Venice. Motorway as far as Trient.
- From Zürich over the St Gotthard Pass, then through Milan, Bergamo, Verona, Padua, Venice. Partly on the motorway in Switzerland, all the way on the motorway in Italy. There are toll charges on all motorways in Italy.

A driving licence and vehicle registration documents, a warning triangle and country stickers are compulsory. The international green insurance card doesn't have to be shown at the border but is advisable in case of accident; comprehensive cover is recommended.

The maximum speed allowed on Italy's toll motorways is 130kmph (80mph) for cars with capacities of over 1.1 litres; smaller vehicles may not travel faster than 110kmph (68mph); and the usual limit on country roads is 90kmph (56mph). Seat belts are compulsory in Italy.

Getting Around

Parking

Waterbus No 82 connects the car park on the island of Tronchetto with San Marco and the Lido. Nos 1, 52, 82, N (night) and 4 (in the summer) link Piazzale Roma (the most central car park) to San Marco and the Lido. In the peak season between June and September there are also extra car parks at Fusina and San Giuliano; line 16 serves Fusina–Zattere all year round.

Water traffic in the lagoon

Enjoying the sights

The most important water-bus connections all connect with the Piazzale Roma, where all land vehicles have to turn back. Tickets can be bought at the small kiosk; large baggage costs extra. One item of hand-luggage, however, is included in the cheaper 24-hour and 3-day tickets.

Line 1 operates the whole year round along the Canal Grande from Tronchetto to Lido; it is supplemented by line 82 as far as San Zaccaria (and to the Lido in season), but the latter line does not stop everywhere. The section in the Canal Grande is described in Route 2 (*see page 31*).

Line 52 and 52 take a circular route around the city centre in both directions (*circolare destra* – round to the right, *circolare sinistra* – round to the left) and are ideal for a city round trip (*see opposite page*). Line 3 is a seasonal route from Tronchetto down the Grand Canal to San Zaccaria and returning via the Giudecca Canal. Line 4 is the reverse of Line 3, starting at San Zaccaria, but passing the Lido on the way back.

Accademia landing stage

The lines that operate to the northern and southern parts of the lagoon are described in the *Excursions* section (*see page 77*). There is also a year-round direct bus connection with Chioggia from the Piazzale Roma. Line 14 operates all year round from Riva Schiavoni via Lido to Punta Sabbioni, where there is a bus connection to Jesolo. Both Punta Sabbioni and Lido are served by the line 17 car ferry which operates the whole year round from Tronchetto.

The main lines run non-stop, but there are not so many boats at night – timetables are posted at all landing-stages and are available at the ACTV offices at Ponte dei Fuseri and at Piazzale Roma (ACTV tel: 041 528 7886).

A trip to Padua on the 'Burchiello'

Today's 'Burchiello' motor-launch is only related in name to the historic ship which used to take a day to reach Padua via the Brenta Canal two centuries ago. The trip includes a visit to the magnificent villas lining the banks of the canal (eg Malcontenta by Palladio, Villa Nazionale in Stra). The service operates from April to October three days a week (usually Tuesday, Thursday and Saturday).

Venice and its gondolas

The gondolas have been black only since 1562, when they became so over-ornate (due to the city's wealthy families' continuous attempts to upstage one another) that a law was passed; as a means of transport, though, they have been in use ever since the time of the first doges (697). They are 10.15m (33.3ft) long and 1.40m (4.6ft) wide, and also 24cm (9.5 inches) shorter on their right-hand side – a peculiarity explained by the fact that the gondolier only places his pole in the water on the right in order to steer. The prow is decorated with a curious toothed projection called the *ferro*, with six strips that are meant to symbolise the six *sestieri* (districts) into which Venice was divided in 1169; the seventh one, pointing in another direction, stands for the island of Giudecca, and the round part is meant to portray the doge's hat. Along certain parts of the Canal Grande the gondola still functions as a *traghetto* (ferry) from one bank to the other. Operating between Rialto fish market and Strada Nuova (Ca' d'Oro); S. Maria del Giglio and Salute; and S. Tomá and Ca' Garzoni (near Palazzo Grassi), they are a great way to save extra walking and only cost 700 lire (for Venetians as well as tourists). The private gondolas are mainly used by visitors eager to discover the city's canals, but, with or without music, during the day or during a romantic evening, Venice wouldn't be the same without a gondola ride.

Gondola service sign

97

City round trips

This may seem an odd idea for a city on the water, but one charming possibility is the *vaporetto* line 52 which goes around the centre, stopping off at San Michele, Murano and La Giudecca. It provides a glimpse of the rather less prestigious *Venezia minore* and also travels through the Arsenal, which was once the largest shipyard in the world (*see page 70*).

Gondola scene

Facts for the Visitor

Travel documents
Visitors from the US, EU and Commonwealth countries need only a passport for a stay of up to three months. Citizens of other countries should check with the nearest Italian consulate about obtaining a visa before travelling.

Customs
You're allowed to bring in as much currency as you like. Non-EU members can bring 400 cigarettes, one bottle of spirits, two of wine and 50g of perfume; EU-members no longer have to declare goods. Non EU-citizens can claim back VAT (IVA). Look out for shops saying *tax free for tourists*.

Currency Regulations
There is no limit on the amount of lire that can be taken in to or out of the country, although for cash transactions there is a restriction of 20 million lire. This also applies within Italy itself.

Information
Information can be obtained from the offices of the Italian State Tourist Office (ENIT) at the following addresses:

UK: Italian State Tourist Office, 1 Princes Street, London W1R 8AY, tel: 0171 408 1254; fax: 0171 493 6695

US: Italian Government Tourist Office, 630 5th Avenue, Suite 1565, NY 10111, New York, tel: 212 245 4822; fax: 212 586 9249.

In Venice: Piazza San Marco, 71/F (Ala Napoleonica), tel: 041 529 8740 or 041 528 8727; the railway station; Piazzale Roma (car park); Lido, Gran Viale 6. Hotel porters can provide the free brochure, *Un Ospite di Venezia* (Guest in Venice), which is published monthly in Italian and English. *Venice Pocket*, a free quarterly publicaton in English, can be obtained from the tourist office or you can buy *Venice News* from a news stand.

Bureau de change

Rolling Venice card
Young people between 14 and 30 years of age can obtain this pass for a small fee from the Agenzia Transalpino at the railway station. It provides several discounts and comes with useful booklets on itineraries, sightseeing, cheap accommodation and restaurants. Don't forget to bring a passport-sized photo plus passport.

Banks and exchange
The basic unit of currency is the *lira*, plural *lire* (L). There are coins worth 50, 100, 200 and 500 lire; notes worth 1-, 2-, 5-, 10-, 20-, 50-, 100- and 500-thousand lire.

Bank hours vary, but are generally Monday to Friday 8.30am–1.20pm and one hour in the afternoon from 2.30–3.30pm, but check locally as afternoon opening times vary. Banks close on weekends and holidays. The *bureaux de change* are open during shopping hours. The exchange offices at the airport and railway station open until the evenings and at weekends.

Traveller's cheques and cheques can be changed at most hotels. Bank rates vary but are usually the most favourable. The lowest rate is to be had by using an international money-teller card at the automated 'Bancomat' cash dispensers that can be found at most banks.

Bills
Restaurants, shops and other establishments are required by law (for tax reasons) to issue an official receipt to customers, who should not leave the premises without it.

Tipping
Even though service is now officially included everywhere, tipping is still customary and bills are rounded off.

Opening times
Most fashion, mask and tourist shops are open from 9am–7.30pm. In other shops there is generally a lunch break from 12.30 or 1pm to 3 or 3.30pm. Foodshops are open from 8am–1pm and 5–7.30pm. Saturday is an ordinary working day; some shops close on Monday mornings or Wednesday afternoons.

Chorus churches
A number of Venice's churches (details at tourist information offices) have linked up to form an association called Chorus. You can buy a pass which allows entrance to any six of these churches within a 48-hour period.

99

Post-box

Post
The main Post Office is close to the Rialto Bridge in the Fondaco dei Tedeschi. It is open Monday to Saturday 9am–6.45pm; Sunday 9am–noon. Other post offices, including one just west of Piazza San Marco in the Calle Larga dell' Ascensione, are open Monday to Friday 8.30am–1.30pm. Stamps *(francobolli)* can be purchased from post offices and also from tobacconists *(tabacchi)*.

Telephoning
This can be done from public telephones, either with *gettoni* (phone tokens) or with 100-, 200- and 500-lire coins; phone cards *(carta telefonica)* are also available and can be bought in 5,000, 10,000- and 15,00-sizes at tobacconists, most bars and many news stands. There are pub-

Telephone box

lic phones at the main Post Office (open 24 hours). International dialling codes: Australia 61; UK 44; US and Canada 1. If calling Venice, even from within the city, you must always dial the previous code 041 as part of the number; if calling from abroad, the '0' is retained.

Time
Italy is six hours ahead of US Eastern Standard Time and one hour ahead of Greenwich Mean Time.

Voltage
Usually 220v, occasionally 110v. Safety plugs cannot always be used. Specialist shops can provide adaptors.

Public Holidays
1 January, 6 January, 25 April, 1 May, 15 August, 1 November, 21 November, 8 December, 25/26 December, Good Friday, Easter Monday. If a public holiday happens to fall on a Tuesday or Thursday, the intervening Monday or Friday may also be taken as a holiday.

Police launch

Medical
Visitors from the EU have the right to claim health services available to Italians. UK visitors should obtain Form E111 from a post office prior to departure, but private insurance is also recommended

There is a 24-hour casualty department at Ospedale Civile, Campo dei SS Giovanni e Paolo, tel: 041 523 0000.

Local newspapers and the booklet *Un Ospite di Venezia* list late-night pharmacies. A late-night rota is also shown on the door of every pharmacy.

Theft and other emergencies
Venice is one of the safest cities in Europe but you should nevertheless watch your valuables in crowded places, especially on the *vaporetti*. It is best to leave valuables in the hotel safe and carry money on you rather than in a shoulderbag or handbag.

In case of theft head immediately to the police (*Questura*) to make an official declaration. A lost passport should be reported to your consulate.

Medical emergency, tel: 118; **all emergencies**, tel: 113; **police emergency**, tel: 112; **police general**, San Marco 996 (off Calle dei Fabri), tel: 041 522 5434.

Lost and found
Lost property offices *(uffici oggetti rinvenuti)* are in the Town Hall, Palazzo Loredan, Riva del Carbon, San Marco (Monday to Friday 8am–2pm); at the station (daily 8am–noon and 3–6pm); at the ACTV office, Piazzale Roma, daily 7.30am–12.30pm or tel: 041 528 7886.

Accommodation

Venice is one of those cities that always has tourists stay-ing, whatever the time of year, and the accommodation sit-uation has developed to cope with this; timely booking is still advisable, though, especially for the summer sea-son, Easter, Whitsun, Carnival and during the Biennale Film Festival (end of August and early September). In Venice, the difference between luxury accommodation and the simple *locanda* (boarding-house) is the same as every-where else; simpler places can entail some surprises, some pleasant, some not so pleasant. It's always a good idea to take a look at the room first – this is quite acceptable in Italy. Nothing is cheap in Venice or on the island of Lido, and that includes overnight accommodation; anyone who decides to stay on the mainland will save a great deal of money.

Hotels in Venice

Hotels *(alberghi)* in Venice are officially classed into five categories: luxury hotels $$$$$; category I $$$$; category II $$$; category III $$; and category IV $.

$$$$$

Cipriani, Giudecca 10, tel: 041 520 7744. On the island of Giudecca with private launch to run you to San Marco. The ultimate in luxury, with 54 rooms, 50 suites, luxuri-ant gardens and an Olympic-size pool (closed Decem-ber to April). **Hotel Danieli**, Riva degli Schiavoni, Castello 4196, tel: 041 522 6480. Two hundred and thirty-eight rooms in an old Gothic palazzo with superb views across the lagoon. Dickens, Wagner, Ruskin and Balzac are among the names on the guest list. **Gritti Palace**, Campo S Maria del Giglio, San Marco 2467, tel: 041 794611. Eighty-eight rooms in the former private palazzo of Doge Andrea Gritti overlooking the Canal Grande. Room 10 is where Hemingway stayed. Generally considered to be the most exclusive hotel in Venice.

$$$$

Londra Palace, Riva degli Schiavoni, Castello 4171, tel: 041 520 0533. Sixty-nine rooms and '100 windows overlooking the lagoon'. A comfortable, civilised hotel with club-style bar, French restaurant and excellent afternoon teas. **Hotel Monaco & Grand Canal**, Calle Val-laresso, San Marco 1325, tel: 041 520 0211. Seventy-five rooms; exceptional setting on the Canal Grande. **Saturnia & International**, Calle Larga XXII Marzo, San Marco 2398, tel: 041 520 8377. Ninety-five rooms in an old palazzo on a smart shopping street close to Piazza San Marco.

Musicians in Piazza San Marco

Restaurant terrace near Ponte dell'Accademia

$$$

Abbazia, Calle Priuli, Cannaregio 66–8, tel: 041 717333. Converted monastery with thirty-six rooms and garden. Within easy reach of Piazzale Roma or the railway station. **Accademia Villa Maravege**, Fondamenta Bollani, Dorsoduro 1058–60, tel: 041 521 0188. Twenty-seven rooms in a quiet location (close to the Accademia gallery). **Do Pozzi**, Calle Larga XXII Marzo, San Marco 2373, tel: 041 520 7855. Twenty-nine rooms, small and spruce hotel in a quiet cul-de-sac conveniently close to Piazza San Marco. Canal-side tables in the adjoining restaurant. **La Fenice et des Artistes**. Campiello de la Fenice, San Marco 1936, tel: 041 523 2333. Sixty-five rooms, many of which used to be taken by performers at the neighbouring Fenice opera house before the fire; still plenty of charm and character. **Flora**, Calle Larga XXII Marzo, San Marco 2283A, tel: 041 520 5844. Forty-four rooms. One of the most desirable small hotels in Venice with quiet garden, pretty décor and location close to Piazza San Marco. **San Moisè**, San Marco 2058, tel: 041 520 3755. Sixteen rooms, on canal near Fenice opera house. Small, friendly and quiet, with traditional Venetian style fabrics and furnishings. Very convenient for Piazza San Marco.

$$–$

Agli Alboretti, Rio Terrà Sant'Agnese, Dorsoduro 884, tel: 041 523 0058. Nineteen rooms. Simple and homely, close to Accademia gallery. **Bucintoro**, Riva San Biagio, Castello 2135, tel: 041 522 3240. Twenty-eight rooms. Good-value, friendly *pensione* right on the waterfront near the Arsenale. Simple rooms with splendid views of the lagoon.**Calcina**, Zattere, Dorsoduro 780, tel: 041 520 6466. Thirty-seven rooms, many looking across the island of Giudecca. Poet John Ruskin stayed here. **Paganelli**, Riva degli Schiavoni, Castello 4182, tel: 041 522 4324. Twenty-two rooms, 3 without bathroom. A modest, well-situated hotel, overlooking the lagoon and a quiet campo. **Locanda Fiorita**, Campiello Nuovo, San Marco 3457, tel: 041 523 4754. Ten rooms. Simple comforts and friendly service, on a small square behind Campo Santo Stefano. **La Residenza**, Campo Bandiera e Moro, Castello 3608, tel: 041 528 5315. Seventeen rooms, in a handsome 15th-century Venetian Gothic palazzo overlooking small square close to the Riva degli Schiavoni. Very much appeals to the independent traveller. **San Fantin**, Campiello Fenice, San Marco 1930A, tel: 041 523 1401. Fourteen rooms. Simple, homely and very handy for the ruins of Fenice opera house. **Seguso**, Zattere, Dorsoduro 779, tel: 041 528 6858. Thirty-six rooms. Pensione which appeals, particularly to the British and French holidaymakers for its charm and splendid views across the Giudecca.